MENTAL MODELS

Problem-solving, Improving your Life, and
your Decision-Making Process, through
the Implementation of Strategic Thinking
and the Right Mental Models

EMILY TAYLOR

Table of Contents

Introduction

Ultimately, the reason people succeed does not have anything to do with their intelligence or work ethic. Even if someone knows more facts than anyone in the world, these facts are useless without having a way to be applied to their lives. Mental models are frameworks that can be used to help you better understand the world around you. By plugging this information you have into a mental model, it allows you to clearly work through the problem or decision. After thinking things through, then you can feel confident you have made the best decision with the greatest chance of a favorable outcome.

Put simply, 'mental model' describes the way that you think. Have you ever been trying to remember someone's name or a word or an important date and felt like you knew the answer, but you just couldn't bring that answer forward from your brain? In these situations, you do not forget—just the route to that information in your brain is temporarily unavailable. Later, by thinking about it in a different way (and usually when you aren't thinking about it at all), you usually remember what you couldn't bring forward. Mental models are also like this. They change the way you think, so information becomes more useful when you need it.

Simply put, mental models are the way you interpret the world. Many people aren't aware that so many mental models govern the way they think, learn, and interpret the world around them. There are many ways that your mind uses mental models to organize information and make it useful, including categories, identities, prototypes, causal narratives, stereotypes, and general worldviews. Mental models are the reason that a group of people can look at the same problem and come up with a different solution. However, the strength when problem-solving or decision making comes from having that group of outcomes. The people who are most successful are those who can come up with the most 'best' outcomes and then logically think through these outcomes to make the best choice.

Even though mental models are incredibly helpful, they can also be limiting. The mental models you use is limited to the mental models you are familiar with. Often, the mental models a person uses most frequently are those associated with their job and those that they use to make decisions in their personal life. They can be formed based on life experience or societal expectations. Mental models (like stereotypes against certain people) can also be passed down from parents to children.

Being aware of the mental models you are familiar with has several benefits. First, it allows you to evaluate them critically and be sure they are serving you. For example, a person might have an ingrained dislike for a group of people because of their parents' attitude toward them. By being aware of this mental model, they could consciously work to overcome it and change the way they think, removing bias from their decisions in life. Second, being aware of mental models gives you a greater range of tools for problem-solving and decision-making. With more tools, you can choose the mental model to use and come up with the greatest range of outcomes. Finally, being aware of mental models helps remove bias from thinking. When decisions are made out of bias rather than based on fact, the outcome is rarely what is expected.

By becoming aware of mental models and learning more, you give yourself the ability to think greatly. You'll feel confident in your ability to make decisions and solve problems, both at work and in your day-to-day life. There isn't a single person who would not benefit from adding more tools to their toolbox and having a wider range of options at their disposal when thinking—it benefits everyone from successful business owners and CEOs to people who are graduating college and still deciding their path in life.

As you read, this book is going to discuss what exactly mental models are and how they shape your thinking. You'll also hear stories about people like Warren Buffett and his business partner Charlie Munger and influential figures like Jeff Bezos and Elon Musk and how they have used mental models on their journey to success. Then, we'll discuss some of the most useful mental models and how you can apply them to problem-solving, decision-making, and your life to help you achieve your version of success.

Chapter 1:

An Introduction to Mental Models

Mental models are designed to help you understand how the world works. It describes any type of framework, concept, or worldview that allows you to make decisions. You can think of a mental model as a tool—and you would not use a hammer to put a screw into a bookshelf. When making decisions and trying to understand the world around them, people are limited by their available tools. When making decisions, therefore, it is better to have more tools.

Then you can apply those tools to the situation at hand.

Not only do mental models aid in decision-making, but they also guide the way you perceive the world around, thus directly affecting your actions. Of course, mental models are flawed in the way they limit the way you view a scenario. It does not matter how many mental models you are aware of if you cannot utilize them in a way that produces the results you are looking for. It is not necessarily a test of who knows the most mental models, but of who can utilize them the best. For day-to-day life, the best mental models are going to be those that can be applied to the widest variety of scenarios. Even then, however, you'll have to pick and choose which are going to allow you to critically analyze the situation in front of you and think rationally, clearly, and effectively.

Where Do Mental Models Come From?

Mental models are a collection of those thinking habits that people form over their lifetime. Some are innate because they come from a social and societal standpoint, such as the idea that incest is wrong. People generally have an aversion to incest without being told to think that way. Others are developed as the result of an upbringing. For example, while racism is generally considered wrong, it is a problem even today because racist beliefs are passed down through generations and many people are not aware of their ability to overcome the bias, so they accept it as being true. A person's environment heavily influences these types of mental models, which is the reason they may vary from society to society.

Other mental models come from an individual's experiences and the way those experiences have shaped their perception of the world. For example, someone who has had several partners be unfaithful might see certain behaviors in their new partner and attribute those to cheating habits, even without evidence that their partner is cheating. Because their learned mental models tell them that their partner is exhibiting similar behaviors, they make assumptions that can be damaging to the relationship.

Learning to identify the mental models you use most is essential for learning to problem solve and think clearly. Even though mental models are at the heart of thought and action, those that are poorly adapted to the task at hand are less likely to produce desirable outcomes than those that have been carefully selected. They also fail where they limit the amount of information considered when making a decision or solving a problem, especially when incorrect assumptions are made. These assumptions are often the result of a person's experiences and how it has shaped the way they perceive the world.

Chapter 2:

A Brief History of Mental Models and Influential Figures Who Have Used Them

The idea of a mental model has existed since the late 1800s, mentioning mental models as representations of ideas. By becoming more familiar with your mental models, there is a greater chance of success in problem-solving, decision-making, and life in general. Before we jump into some principles you'll need to remember when applying various mental models, let's take a look at the history of mental models and how they have been used by some more influential people in the world today.

A Brief History of Mental Models

American philosopher Charles Sanders Peirce is credited with the earliest ideas of mental models, or the psychological representation of ideas that are real, imaginary, or hypothetical. In an 1896 book, Peirce explored the idea of reasoning, which is a type of mental model. He stated that it was a process where a person "examines the state of things asserted in the premisses, forms a diagram of that state of things, perceives in the parts of the diagram relations not explicitly mentioned in the premisses, satisfies itself by mental experiments upon the diagram that these relations would always subsist, or at least would do so in a certain proportion of cases, and concludes their necessary, or probable, truth."

Others also explored the idea of mental models in their writing. Kenneth Craik, a Scottish psychologist, wrote in his book that the mind uses small-scale models of real situations. These pieces of reality are used to reason, prepare for events, and find underlying explanations. Each mental model is designed with a structure that is related to the structure of the situation it represents. For example, an architect making a model scale of a building is a mental model, a type of visualization that is crafted after the same real-life or hypothetical building that it is intended to represent.

Since Craik, others have weighed in on the idea of mental models and how they may be applied. Many cognitive scientists have weighed in on the usefulness of mental models, which are heavily affected by a person's perceptions and feelings about a situation.

Physicist Richard Feynman is another noted for his work with mental models. When he was working to receive his Ph.D. from Princeton and his undergraduate degree from MIT, he was often known for visiting the math department and solving problems—even those math problems that the Ph.D. students were incapable of solving. His secret? Feynman had learned a strategy in high school physics class that changed his life.

After noting that Feynman talked and moved around too much in class, his teacher spoke to him after school about his problem—Feynman was bored. Then, he gave him a book to study during class—Advanced Calculus by Woods. His teacher told him to sit in the corner during lessons and not to speak, instead of studying the book until he had learned everything in it. During that time, Feynman began developing mental models. He taught himself how to use an integral sign to develop and differentiate parameters. Though the integral method is not commonly used in graduate classes, Feynman had mastered it. He was able to solve those problems not because he had more intelligence but because he had a different set of tools that the Ph.D. math students. This broader set of tools let him see problems differently, thus leading him to the solution.

Mental Models Through History

Historians maintain that the Renaissance and Enlightenment both represent major shifts in the beliefs at the time. The Renaissance happened between the 14th and 17th centuries. Prior to the Renaissance, there was a heavy focus on religion. Events like the Black Death that killed an estimated 75-200 million people across Europe left people feeling as if God were unjust. There was a greater separation between church and state and the ideas of the time focused more on the enjoyment of life and exploring the world. It was during this time that writing, art, philosophy, and the sciences became popular as humans sought after a greater understanding.

The Enlightenment period also reflected a shift in societal attitudes and ideas that could also be considered a change in mental models. There was greater support for the idea that humans exist under universal physical laws rather than exist to please a divine being. The discovery of physical laws made many new ideas capable, including mass production technology and change in economic structures. These changes allowed people to think about the world around them in new ways, broadening their mental models and allowing great exploration into areas like math, engineering, and the sciences.

Influential Figures Who Have Used Mental Models

Many people who have risen to success, including Jeff Bezos, Warren Buffett, Charlie Munger, and Elon Musk attribute some of their great success to their ability to think and learn.

Warren Buffett, Charlie Munger, and Mental Models
Warren Buffett is well-known for his prowess as an investor, though his business partner Charlie Munger is given less credit. Munger is more out of the financial spotlight but is known for his extensive work in organizing mental models. One of the most famous speeches regarding mental models was given by Charlie Munger at USC Business School in 1994. Even though the speech was intended to discuss his business philosophy and investment, he also discussed a general framework for wise decision making. It is this type of decision making that sets success apart from failure. Business partner Warren Buffett had also used these mental models, which allowed both to become learning machines. They took the time to attack problems from different angles before choosing a solution, which allowed them to make the wisest and most effective business decisions.

The models used by people like Buffett and Munger are rules of thumb that create a truth that can be generally accepted by the majority. Therefore, any information that can be put into a specific mental model lets the problem evaluated from a certain angle. With several mental models available to analyze any given problem, a person can reduce the amount of uncertainty in their world and feel assured that the decisions they are making are those that are going to yield the best result.

In a way, mental models make a person smarter. This is not merely a collection of knowledge or ideas, but the way that knowledge and ideas are applied to the decision-making process. People often take the complexity that exists around them for granted, never truly realizing the impact that it has on their lives. People are generally focused on 1-2 factors and the results that it will produce. In reality, however, there could be billions of variables that affect a single situation. People see surface-level results because they do not account for these extra variables. However, the solution isn't to account for all those variables. There are so many variables that can influence a situation that it may be impossible to know which of these variables to focus on to sway the outcome the way you are hoping. Additionally, it would be impossible to sway every single variable that comes into play in a situation. Instead of overburdening your brain with these minute details, people rely on mental models.

Even though there is no single perfect model, perfection is not necessary for a mental model to work. They are merely a tool that makes all those complex variables that surround a decision easier to account for.

According to Munger, it is essential that a person looks for mastery of mental models across different disciplines. Some of the areas Munger has studied and learned the principles of include accounting, physics, psychology, finance, economics, architecture, medicine, mathematics, history, geography, sociology, biology, and chemistry. The reasoning behind this is that there are elements of every discipline that can contribute to a person's collection of mental models. Even though people agree, there are some mental models that are more helpful than others and more easily able to be applied to life, not all of these mental models exist within the same academic department. People's mental models are often flawed because they specialize in a single area. For example, business people make decisions according to certain principles that they use to evaluate risks and benefits. Someone who is a researcher or scientist may use hypothesis or experiments to solve problems. It is not necessarily a bad thing, however, it limits a person's ability to see the full scope of possibilities when problem-solving and decision-making.

Something else to keep in mind is that the same mental models do not work for everyone. It would be nearly impossible to master dozens of disciplines to the extent needed to handle some of the more complex mental models. Fortunately, the most useful models are those based on simplicity rather than complex ideas. You do not have to master a discipline to master some of its basic principles. Even a basic foundation in different disciplines allow you to view problems and decision-making from new angles, giving you a greater range of options and a better chance of success.

As you learn about the variety of mental models available, it's important that you decide which are most useful. Some mental models are best used to create a framework, while others are usable simply by being aware of them.

Elon Musk and Mental Models

Many people consider Elon Musk's list of accomplishments incredible. Though he is only in his mid-40s, he already has four successful companies in fields including software, transportation, energy, and aerospace. Many people credit this incredible feat to his 80+ hour work weeks, goal-setting, and resilience, however, many people have these things and it is not enough to propel them to the same level of success. One thing that Musk does have that others lack is an understanding of many disciplines. He has mastered many disciplines in his lifetime, including areas like rocket science, physics, engineering, construction, artificial intelligence, solar power, and energy.

One of the reasons Elon Musk has been able to dedicate so much time to his overall success is because he is a polymath. These are people who study widely in different fields for a minimum of five hours each week. By giving themselves time to study each of these disciplines, they understand the deeper principles and mental models that interlink the various fields. As more information and more mental models are collected, they can be applied to a person's chosen core specialty.

What can be learned from polymaths like Elon Musk is that there is a benefit to learning more than one field. One famous saying says, "Jack of all trades, master of none." If you look at the many polymaths that have achieved success today, however, it is clear that is not true. These people have advantages from learning across many fields, including:

- A world-class skillset built by combining atypical skills
- Increased information advantage
- Improved chance of success in your career
- Greater perspective in different areas
- Separation from the global economy

You see, when you specialize in more than one field, there is an overlap of the ideas you can produce. A person in the tech industry who knows a lot about biology might apply that information to come up with unique ideas. According to Musk, the key to success in many disciplines is studying them and then using what is called learning transfer.

Learning transfer involves taking what is learned in one area and then applying it to another, whether it is the real world or another industry. When these core ideas are combined, it gives a wider range of decision making and problem-solving strategies.

Among Musk's many strategies is the technique of extracting mental models and principles from those subjects learned. Rather than focusing on a single idea or fact, the information is broken down into easier-to-manage parts.

To break this information down into core principles, it's best to have other core principles to compare it against. This is the major benefit of the multi-disciplinary approach. When the same cases are looked at, it is nearly impossible to break the information down in a way that is manageable. By looking at different cases across multiple disciplines, the information and core principles become significantly clearer. It is also easier to learn with the links between the different pieces of information.

Let's take a look at how Elon Musk applies this. Among the fields that he has mastered the foundational principles of are technology, physics, artificial intelligence, and engineering. Then, these subjects were applied to different ideas like self-driving Tesla and SpaceX. The easiest way to compare these ideas is to think about what each principle reminds you of. Instead of focusing only on the subject you are learning, think about how the topic can be applied to other areas you are knowledgeable in. Then, consider why it reminds you of this subject and make the connection.

Jeff Bezos and Mental Models

Before Jeff Bezos started Amazon, he used the regret minimization framework of thinking. Bezos had a great idea, but he was not yet confident enough to take that leap and create Amazon. The initial idea was to create an online store that sold books. Everyone he talked to thought it was a great idea, however, his boss pushed it to the side. After all, Bezos already had a good, high-paying job—what was the point of taking the risk?

The regret minimization framework comes into play because it gave Bezos an effective way to visualize the possibility of the idea. He spent just 48 hours making the decision that would change his life. The regret minimization is simple. Ask yourself, "Will I regret not doing this in X years?" If Bezos had never brought his business to fruition, he never would have developed Amazon, a corporation that would grow exponentially after its conception.

To effectively use this model, it's important to visualize the future and then look back. If you are not going to regret not doing something, don't bother investing your time with it. If there is a chance of regret, it is better to follow through on the plans and make it a reality. Bezos said:

"I knew that when I was 80 I was not going to regret having tried this. I was not going to regret trying to participate in this thing called the Internet that I thought was going to be a really big deal. I knew that if I failed I wouldn't regret it, but I knew the one thing I might regret is never having tried."

The major benefit of the regret minimization as you can see is that it forces you to propel yourself forward and look beyond the present moment. By looking back from this future setting, you can assess from a new perspective. This perspective allows a better evaluation of the decision and possible outcomes.

How You Can Use Mental Models to Change Your Life

As you can see, some of the most influential and successful people in the world have relied on mental models. Buffett and Munger are known for using mental models to make solid investments, looking over potential investments for key signs that they could have exponential growth. Elon Musk studies mental models and basic principles across many disciplines, using his wide breadth of knowledge to come up with innovative ideas. Finally, even Jeff Bezos has used mental models in decision making, helping him decide to launch an incredibly successful company.

Even though all these people have an incredible work ethic, they are constantly collecting information and analyzing it using the various mental models at their disposal. Using the same techniques, you too can begin changing your reality.

Something that is true is that life is based on cause-and-effect. Even when you do not have a clear picture of the outcomes of your decision, it is your decisions that set things in motion. If Jeff Bezos had never decided to take that risk and launch the company, somebody else may have launched Amazon and his life would likely be very different.

The same is true for problem-solving. When solving problems, you are limited to those options that you can see. It is impossible to solve a problem with a solution that you have not come up with yet. By learning the basic principles of various fields, there is a wider range of solutions that you can use to problem-solve. This gives the best possible outcome of success. As your problem-solving and decision-making skills improve, you'll ultimately learn how to choose the life that you want and begin living it. Anything becomes possible.

Building a Latticework of Mental Models

It is not enough to memorize sheets of mental models and hope they stick. In fact, it is better to focus on learning a single discipline at a time. Choose various subjects and explore the principles, focusing on that discipline and its ideas until you understand its core latticework and how it relates to other principles you have studied. According to Charlie Munger:

"You have to learn all the big ideas in the key disciplines in a way that they're a mental latticework in your head and you automatically use them for the rest of your life."

A good way to think of building mental models is by imagining a house. Before you can start using mental models and understanding how they connect to other areas you have studied, you need a solid foundation. From there, you'll build a supporting structure and put in electrical wiring and plumbing. Like a house, you want your mental models to be well-built and something that you can use for years to come. In addition to studying the various disciplines, it is necessary to tie the ideas together in a way that makes them more useful together than they would be alone.

Chapter 3:

General Guidelines and Techniques for Applying Mental Models

To properly apply mental models, regardless of the type of mental model, there are certain guidelines that can be used. Before you take a look at the next chapters that will discuss some of the mental models that will benefit you most in your life, take a look at this chapter. As you learn new models, these same guidelines will be applied. Use this as a framework to build upon your mental models' skills box.

#1: First Principles Thinking

The first principles thinking guideline describes the use of creative possibility in mental models. Before you begin clarifying complicated problems, it is important to separate those things that are facts and any underlying ideas from the assumptions derived from the situation. Once the assumptions are removed, only the bits of information that can be applied to the situation are used. Then, you can begin seeking the additional information that you need to make an informed and wise decision based on what you know instead of what you think you know.

#2: Remember Maps are Imperfect

Even the most meticulous map designers can make maps that are imperfect, If a map were perfect, it would not be a reduction—it would be a whole. Additionally, as time goes on, territories often change, which makes the map less accurate. Maps may even be representative of something that no longer exists. As you apply various mental models, it is important to remember that the map can change. It is not a perfect representation of the territory or the boundaries of your situation, and this should be accounted for as you look for alternative decisions and solutions for problems.

#3: Second-Order Thinking

Second-order thinking allows people to move past their initial conclusions in the short-term and focus on the long-term. If two people use the same mental model with the same inputs and information, odds are they will reach the same first-order conclusion. This conclusion is usually easier to reach. People who think more creatively go beyond that, looking at the situation as a whole and considering both long-term and short-term results. Therefore, it's important to remember that not all mental models are like math. There is not always one, single answer and it is important to consider second- and third-order effects of any decisions you make or conclusions you draw.

#4: Thought Experiments

Thought experiments are tools of exploration that allow you to examine the deeper nature of something. For example, fields of study like physics and philosophy often require someone to take a deeper look at what knowledge is and is not known. Thought experiments are used to examine new ways to apply what is known. When using mental models, it is important to examine what is known about the historical use of the models and inputs. By learning from mistakes in the past, it allows for a clearer evaluation of mental models in the future.

#5: Consider Your Competence

One of the biggest things that holds people back from proper problem-solving and decision-making is their inability to analyze their own flaws. There is no single person that possesses all the knowledge in the world, or that is always right. True power when using mental models comes from an ability to see the bigger picture and where your knowledge is lacking. By identifying strengths and weaknesses, a person can be aware of the areas where they need to learn more. This is known as the circle of competence, and by becoming more understanding of this circle, decision-making and outcomes are significantly improved.

#6: Inversion

The inversion technique helps you remove obstacles when solving a problem. Instead of diving into the problem, you look at in the opposite way that people typically would. Since people commonly only look at a situation forward, it helps work through the problem without the same roadblocks. We'll take a closer look at inverted thinking as we explore some of the mental models in later chapters.

#7: Probabilistic Thinking

This type of thinking involves using tools of logic and math to estimate the likelihood of a specific outcome. When you use mental models, there are not always clear outcomes. There may be unstable elements of a mental model or things that cannot be calculated. For example, a person may use a mental model to draw conclusions about breaking bad news to someone. Even though they can plan for the person's possible reactions and estimate the probability of how they will react, there are still many complex factors that must be considered. By considering the probability of each reaction, the decision made would be more effective and precise.

Often, probabilistic thinking has two process—fat-tailed processes and Bayesian updating. Fat-tailed processes place heavier emphasis on the possibility of what would otherwise be considered outlier events. By giving them more focus, the strategies used become riskier or more profitable. Generally, a fat tail on the negative side indicates risk and a fat tail on the positive side has more benefits or a greater chance of possibilities. This strategy is often applied to the human social world, which as a greater chance of the outliers occurring.

Bayesian updating involves taking all information previously known into account first. Then, as new information becomes available, the mental model is updated in increments. This is an especially effective method, as it allows people to combine what they know from previous situations with any new information to draw the best possible conclusion at a point in time.

#8: Hanlon's Razor

This principle states that people should attribute things as being derived from bad intent when the easier solution is stupidity. Ideology and paranoia are major factors in the social world, however, people are incredibly flawed. It is much more likely that someone acts out of carelessness or stupidity than acting maliciously without reason. By looking at things in this frame, it allows mental models to be created separately from the emotions and assumptions associated with them. Generally, the solution is whichever solution provides the least intent from the offending party.

#9: Occam's Razor

Generally, simpler explanations are considered truer than complicated ones. This is based on the principle that it is better for an explanation to have fewer moving parts. Without extra factors, it becomes easier for a person to decide confidently. Additionally, it prevents time wasted disproving complex scenarios.

#10: Learn to Challenge Your Mental Models

Even though it is useful to have a wide variety of mental models at your disposal, this does not necessarily mean all your mental models are useful. One famous account of how mental models can be erroneous comes from Nelson Mandela, the first South African black president, as well as politician, philanthropist, and social rights activist. While traveling from Sudan to Ethiopia, Mandela noticed that the pilot was black, and as he had never seen a black man fly an airplane before, he felt a sense of panic. Mandela's panic did not serve him in any way, which means that mental model and the stigma that he had against the black pilot also did not serve him. The problem is that many people lack the ability to critically evaluate their own mental models and do away with those that do not serve them. In fact, they may go out of their way to ignore information that disproves their theories and their worldviews in any way. In this case, a mental model becomes an obstacle rather than a tool that can be used to create positive outcomes when problem-solving and decision making.

As you learn the various mental models in this book, it is important to keep these basic principles in mind. These principles will help guide you in a new way of thinking and make mental models easier to access.

Chapter 4:

Putting Mental Models into Perspective: What They Are and What They Are Not

Even though mental models are undoubtedly useful, they are not the 'keys to the kingdom' on their own. Mental models are meant to give you a clearer picture of reality. Unfortunately, many people distort this picture based on their own experiences. While storing information about the experiences we have is important, it can also create bias. To properly use mental models, it is important that these biases are identified and accounted for. Otherwise, the mental model is as flawed as the bias that is influencing it, and it becomes harder to accurately predict outcomes.

This chapter will help you understand what mental models are and what they are not, which will help you decide how they can be best applied in life.

"We all have mental models: the lens through which we see the world that drives our responses to everything we experience. Being aware of your mental models is key to being objective."

-Elizabeth Thorton

Mental models are not foolproof in their ability to map the world. They are subject to human error and rarely detail the reality of the situation. However, once you become more aware of the mental models you use and their likelihood of yielding either satisfying or dissatisfying thoughts, you can begin picking and choosing the mental model that will work best in the situation. In order to do that, it is important to be aware of each model's strengths and where it falls short.

For example, imagine that you were solving a complex math problem. You could go through hundreds of equations, but unless the right equation was applied to the problem, it would not yield a satisfying (or accurate) solution.

Cause-and-Effect in Problem Solving

In many ways, the human mind is a double-edged sword. Even though it quickly evaluates cause and effect, this quick evaluation often causes the mind to overlook important variables. This isn't to say that you must think of and evaluate the billions of elements that come together when faced with a problem or decision. However, it is important to account for different factors that will significantly impact the result.

The major benefit of this quick cause-and-effect evaluation that the mind does is that it creates order in the brain and lets you draw conclusions in a logical way; in a way that makes sense. Unfortunately, even though the brain's own cause-and-effect is similar to a mental model in its usefulness, it is also similar to a mental model in the way that it is flawed. Cause-and-effect relationships are a shortcut, and it is not uncommon for these shortcuts to be misguided or wrong. They are based on instinct and subconscious thought rather than the rationalities (or lack of rationalities) in the situation.

Blind Spots and Mental Models

Among Munger's theories regarding mental models is the idea that people can limit the risks or potential downsides of a situation by avoiding mistakes instead of focusing on coming up with the most brilliant solution. Even solutions that take many factors into account expose a person to some harm. Eventually, regardless of a person's brilliance, their tendency to take risks is going to result in poor luck. It is not a matter of intelligence, but of statistics and the reality that there is no single person that is right all the time. People naturally develop blind spots. These are connections, factors, and other elements that are easily overlooked, whether a person ignores them or they do not have experience with them.

Once a person acknowledges the blind spots that exist in the mental models they use in day-to-day lives, they can learn to identify and account for these blind spots. For example, people often experience confirmation bias, which means they have a tendency to choose evidence depending on what supports their ideas rather than looking for the truth. When a person recognizes this bias, they can take a more critical look at the information and thus create a more accurate and effective mental model.

Mental Models Can Be Useful or Limiting

One of the biggest struggles when examining the tools in our toolbox is having a limited view of the world. For example, someone who works as a divorce lawyer may overanalyze the relationships they try to have because they see divorce everywhere. While this is good insight when it comes to identifying problems in a relationship, it can also cause the person to look for problems. If the divorce lawyer is constantly looking for problems in their personal relationships, especially problems that have ultimately caused the end for many of their clients, they will always struggle to be happy in a relationship. They may find it hard to be committed since they see so many commitments failing day in and day out.

Essentially, for mental models to work well, they have to be used in a way that is beneficial. With the divorce lawyer, if they are always nitpicking problems as a means of an end, rather than recognizing problems and using their insight to handle them, they are ultimately choosing to have an unsuccessful dating life. The key to using mental models properly is to use them in a way that provides the greatest benefit with the lowest risk.

If you put a business executive and an environmental expert in the same room and ask them to discuss what to do with a plot of land, chances are the options will be vast and it will be difficult for the pair to come to a conclusion about anything. The business executive is more likely to focus on the habitat in terms of what it can do for development or how it can turn a profit in some way, while the environmental expert might be focused on improving the natural habitat or the quality of the living environment.

The two would likely come to a head because of what is known as mental models. Put simply, mental models are representations of the world. People use mental models to solve their problems. These mental models are developed over a person's lifetime as they learn new things and recognize patterns in their lives.

Mastery of mental models is a good thing, however, it also has the potential to be someone's downfall. People who rely on a small group of mental models or ways of thinking are ultimately limiting their ability to see the true potential of the situation. It becomes impossible to choose the best possible outcome because they cannot clearly see the reality of the choices in front of them.

It is natural to favor certain mental models, especially when you have become accustomed to thinking in a specific way. Unfortunately, the more you favor any single mental model, the more likely it is that the model will be your downfall. It is easy to get caught in the trap of favoring the mental models most familiar to you. When you are solving problems or making decisions, however, the most desirable outcome is not always what is most familiar to you. If you allow familiarity to dictate what you do, it will be nearly impossible to make the changes that are often required for success. Remember that while expertise can be a good thing, particularly when you are establishing your authority in an area, it can also be a limitation.

Removing Bias from Mental Models

Mental models are incredibly subject to bias. Like with the divorce lawyer, they saw only the bad side of the problems instead of looking for opportunities to fix them. The easiest way to remove bias is to consider only the factual

information that can be proven. This is challenging, especially in personal relationships because it can be hard to remove emotion. This is even true in the workplace. For example, imagine that a person has the opportunity to go away on a week-long trip with work that has the potential to advance the career. However, the person in charge of the trip is someone that they do not get along with at work. They may be biased in their decision of whether to go or not because they might allow their personal relationship with that person to get in the way of accomplishing greater things in their life. However, they are punishing themselves rather than punishing the other person and choosing a path that ultimately leads to a lesser degree of success.

Furthermore, to be truly successful in life, it is critical that you are open to new opinions and ideas. One of the biggest mistakes that people make when sharing ideas with others or having disagreements is that they do not listen. Rather than listening to the other person's ideas and using it to gain a new perspective, they may shut the idea down before it comes to fruition because they do not want to hear anything that contrasts their own beliefs.

In otder to successfully use mental models, these fallacies must be overcome. Learning is a critical part of using all the mental models at your disposal. As you make connections of the principles across different disciplines, you gain a greater understanding of the knowledge available and different methods of thinking. Rather than running from this, it is important to embrace it and remain open-minded to new ideas and new perspectives. After all, with a greater number of outcomes, there is a greater chance of success.

What Mental Models Are Not: A Constant

Mental models do not represent a constant, as they can change as new information or sequences are introduced to the model. The purpose of a mental model is to create a simulation or a representation of what is in front of you. Often, mental models are visual in nature. By adding information into the 'matrix' that is a mental model, the results of the model change.

Even though mental models are used for decision-making and mental processes, they are not definitive by any means. Mental models have limits, such as the information available at the time, a person's unique perception of the situation they are in, and limits based on the mental model itself, as there is no single mental model that can be used to draw conclusions and make decisions—it is a matter of picking and choosing the mental models that can be best applied to the situation at hand.

It is not uncommon for terms like if, and, or to be used to create conditions within a mental model. These conditions allow the scenario to be played out in full and for firm conclusions to be drawn. These terms also help account for deficiencies and problems within the mental models.

What Mental Models Are: Tools for Understanding

Mental models are necessary for evaluating the world around us. The problem is that while the ideal situation involves having a latticework of different mental models, situations are not always ideal. Most people are specialists, which limits our ability to make decisions to those few mental models that we specialize in. Psychologists may think in terms of incentives, as they know people have reasons for acting the way they act. Engineers think in systems, and biologists think about evolution and change. The problem is that by only seeing the situation from a single perspective, it creates a blind spot that allows the situation to be seen clearly and in its full potential.

The problem is that with limited mental models, it is

impossible to see the full scope of something without the ability to see various mental models. Imagine that a group of people was given the task of managing a decaying forest. A business person may only think about the value of the land and whether they should evolve it for business instead of trying to restore the natural habitat. An environmentalist might note the impacts of climate change, while a botanist would be focused on the ecosystem as a whole and the effects of different plants and animals in the area. A forestry engineer may only see the forest in terms of tree growth. Without the ability to share knowledge, however, each of these people is limited in their ability to clearly see the forest, and they cannot get to the true solution in the matter. A better alternative would be for all the disciplines to share their mental models, thus allowing them to see the full picture and come up with the most comprehensive solution.

Charlie Munger explored this idea in a 1990s speech, where he summed up the theory of mental models and the approach of practical wisdom by stating that the first rule is that it is not enough to know isolated facts. It is nearly impossible to remember a series of facts, especially since wisdom does not come from who can remember the most facts. Wisdom comes from taking those facts and hanging them on a latticework of theory to create a usable form. Without models, therefore, the simple memorization of facts means nothing.

Application of Mental Models

As you read, it is important to remember that even though mastering a variety of models is helpful, it is not enough just to have the list of mental models. Mental models have limits. They are not some magical formula that leads you to success in life. In addition to considering bias, you'll need to know how to apply different mental models to come up with new results. As you learn which mental models are most appropriate for your career and life, take the time to study various scenarios and the mental models that can be applied in them. Simply by studying the many ways that mental models can be used, you arm yourself with knowledge on the vast application. Even though there are some that can only be used in certain fields, many mental models can be carried over and used to make better, more favorable decisions in other areas of life as well.

Chapter 5:

Choosing Areas of Focus

Ultimately, your ability to solve problems and make decisions is limited to the mental models that you have at your disposal. If you limit yourself to just a few mental models or mental models within a single discipline, you are greatly limiting your perspective of the world. You are also greatly limiting your ability to look at situations objectively, see the full potential, and make the best possible decisions.

Have you ever been having a conversation with someone and they come up with an idea, and you say, "Why didn't I think of that?" This happens when there is so much focus on a single area that your view is clouded. There is a blind spot where that solution was sitting, so you were incapable of seeing it. Charlie Munger, Warren Buffett, Jeff Bezos, and Elon Musk are all among those who have become more successful in life simply because they saw a wider potential when making decisions about their business (and even their life). With more solutions and choices at their disposal, as well as by having the knowledge and capability to analyze the solutions and choices, it becomes possible to make the decisions that result in success. This chapter will go over some disciplines that you'll want to include in your arsenal. Within these disciplines, there are several mental models that can greatly affect the way you think in other areas of your life as well.

In the next few chapters, the various mental models are going to be laid out according to discipline. It is important to remember that these mental models by no means represent the entire arsenal of models at your disposal.

Studying Across Various Disciplines

Not all mental models are created equally. Some only apply to certain scenarios. For example, the same engineering and physics models that allow people to build bridges and even travel to space will do little in the real world or relationships. Those 'big' mental models are the ones that can be applied broadly to life and decision-making. Investor, philanthropist, and businessman Charlie Munger, who works alongside Warren Buffett, has said, "80 or 90 important models will carry about 90% of the freight in making you a worldly-wise person. And, of those, only a mere handful really carry very heavy freight." Put simply, this means that even though there are hundreds of models, only a few of these models are truly going to have the utility you need in your life and career. Even though it may be a good idea to master these few important models, you'll also want to add more models to your toolbox.

For example, one strategy commonly used by Munger and Buffett while making financial decisions is to look for signs that a company is undervalued compared to its market valuation. Though they may keep a wide portfolio of stocks, the greatest profits come from the small section of companies that the pair recognizes as being a hidden gem compared to current market value. Even though there are many other factors that may be used, they use key principles that they have learned over time, which generally points to the 'truth' that a stock will perform well. By using this filter, they can evaluate investments quicker and make the quick decisions needed for stock market success.

How to Explore Mental Models

The greatest suggestion that can be offered regarding mental models is that developing these models is a matter of practice and commitment. There are hundreds of mental models that can be applied to life, but you cannot have knowledge of these models without studying them. Learning mental models is a process, as they are a comprehensive way to break out of your usual patterns of thought and have a wider range of options available as you consider decisions. However, it takes time to master each of these models. Give each new model time and then add it to your toolbox before moving on to the next one. By focusing on one model at a time, you'll give yourself the ability to properly use it and apply the general guidelines, which will make it applicable to different scenarios in your life.

Many people find it useful to create visual graphics as they explore mental models. As you learn more in fields that seem unrelated, one thing you'll notice is that there are key concepts that have a wide range of applications. Challenge yourself to find the connection between all these different topics and how they overlap. You can also challenge yourself by trying to come up with a scenario for how each mental model could be applied to your life. By studying scenarios, you'll find yourself more prepared when it is time to put the mental models you have learned to use.

Chapter 6:

A Collection of Mental Models Worth Knowing

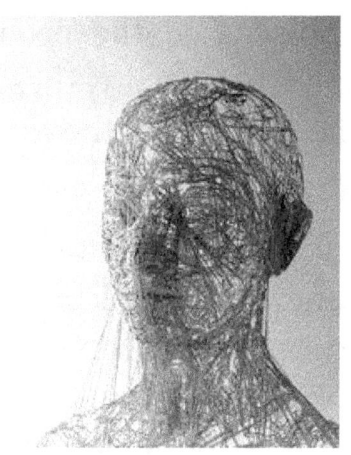

It would be impossible to write a single book that covers all the mental models at your disposal, especially since there are useful mental models across all disciplines. This is the reason that people from different backgrounds are able to solve problems in different ways and come up with unique ideas. Even though it's not possible to list every single mental model, this chapter will include some of the most useful.

The Probability Theory

French scientist Blaise Pascal is quoted as saying:

"Fear of harm ought to be proportional not merely to the gravity of the harm, but also to the probability of the event [occurring]."

In the 1650s, Pascal exchanged a series of letters with mathematician Pierre de Fermat. In these letters, the pair discussed the probability of odds in games of chance. Eventually, these letters would form the basis of the probability theory.

The probability theory is used for those situations that cannot be guaranteed. For example, even if the weatherman predicts rain, you cannot be 100% sure that it is going to rain. Likewise, when playing cards, there is no guarantee that you will be dealt a royal flush. It is possible—the amount that it is possible is the probability.

When making decisions, whether in business or in life, the solution is not always as simple as deciding between the best of two options. In addition to considering all potential outcomes, it's important to consider the likelihood of an outcome happening. For example, imagine that a family decides to go camping. Even though there might be wildlife in the area like bears, the probability of actually getting attacked by a bear is rather low. You can also think of probability as describing randomness. As many situations do not always produce the same outcome, especially since there is an infinite number of factors that contribute to the outcome, there is always randomness that must be accounted for when problem-solving and decision making. By being aware of this randomness and the likelihood that it will occur, a person can determine the reality of the risks and benefits in the situation.

Though probability theory started out as an idea, it would eventually grow to become an entire mathematics field. It was also practical. One of its earlier uses involved calculating the risk of mortality for insurance companies. Probability also has widespread applications in fields like engineering and science.

Using Probability as a Mental Model

As a mental model, probability manages risks. There will always be some areas where you have absolutely no control. Often, these are the areas where you cannot determine cause and effect. When the link is hidden, it becomes almost impossible to truly calculate the risk. The main goal when using the probability mental model, therefore, is finding the balance between those areas you can and cannot control.

For example, imagine that a family wants to go to the zoo on Saturday, but there is a 15% chance of rain. Even though there is a low risk of rain, the family does not want to be unprepared. Instead of forgoing the zoo visit altogether, it might be better to prepare for the rain in case that 15% probability becomes the reality. Ultimately, when making decisions, you want to choose the option that does the most benefit with a low-to-medium risk. The amount of risk you are willing to take should reflect the potential payoff. In the investing world, for example, it is not uncommon for financial investors to take some risks because riskier investments are sometimes the ones with the highest payout. To minimize risks, investors keep a diverse portfolio that contains risky and less-risky prospects.

Even though it is okay (and sometimes necessary) to take risks, the probability theory can be applied by choosing only those decisions and solutions where the risks are minimal enough that there is a more probable chance of success than an unfavorable outcome. Here are a few guidelines to consider for long-term success when using probability mental models:

- Examine many situations- The best way to be prepared for anything is to spend time examining different situations and their outcomes. In the stock market, for example, investors might look for trends or patterns that indicate a company is profitable. The key to examining many situations in whatever area you are focused on is collecting information about the cause-and-effect in each scenario.

- Maintain high focus- Even though you want to collect a wide variety of mental models, to apply them most to your life for success, it's helpful to focus on being an expert in a single area. You should verse yourself in the many disciplines to have a wide range of mental models for solving problems, however, you should apply these disciplines only in certain areas of your life. For example, it is better to focus on your career and your personal life, rather than focusing on improving in areas that do not align with your personal goals. Let's use the example of a person who gambles for a living. A professional gambler does not go into the casino and play slots, some craps, and some blackjack. By focusing on a single area and evaluating risks, they are more likely to have success playing only blackjack or only craps.

- Consider the ante. In something like gambling, you have to play every time you play. Fortunately, this is not the truth for all areas of life. By using the probability mental model, you can first evaluate a situation before deciding how much to ante up. When you can invest less of your time or money and still have a high chance of reward, those are the times when it is best to expend your energy.

- Know your opportunities are limited. Even when someone is successful at something, it is nearly impossible to have positive outcomes 100% of the time. There are rarely times when you will have a clear perception of what needs to be done before you act.

Decision Trees

Decision trees are considered mathematical because of the organized, logical thinking that they facilitate. When creating a decision tree, you explore different outcomes of certain actions. As you go through all the possible scenarios, you can clearly identify potential risk and reward for each decision. With such a logical approach, it is easier to establish cause-and-effect as well.

Using Decision Trees as a Mental Model
The first course of action when creating a decision tree is laying out all the possible options in front of you. Then, list the risks and rewards associated with each decision. In finance or business, it would be easiest to quantify these and choose the option with the most value. As you look over the 'branches' of the tree where the risks and rewards of each option are listed, you'll then calculate the probability of each alternative happening, with the total sum of the numbers for each decision adding up to 100%. Then, choose the decision with the best possible chance of a positive outcome.

Decision trees have the major benefit of helping you truly visualize all the options at your disposal. Additionally, all potential outcomes of each option are considered thoroughly. By assigning monetary values and probability percentages to each possible outcome, it becomes possible for you to make the best possible decision.

Time Value of Money

The time value of money simply states that money on hand today is worth more than the same amount of money received at a future time. This is an important principle in business. When a company has a high liquid value, it possesses many assets that can be converted quickly to cash. These liquid items are considered in a different category as assets like inventory because they are present money that a company has on hand.

Applying the Time Value of Money
It is not uncommon for businesses to offer their customers discounts on money that is paid in advance. For example, a company may process an order for 600 coffee cups at $2 each. The invoice would bill for $1,200, but the company might offer a discount of 2% if the money is paid within a certain timeframe (usually 15-30 days). Even though it may seem like the business is losing money, they are actually encouraging customers to pay early. This means that they have cash on hand sooner and can

then use that available cash to invest in the business or to put away and earn interest.

The time value of money can also be applied to your personal life. For example, imagine that you are saving up for something—to start a new business or buy a new car. Instead of tucking away a little bit of money each week and hoping it is enough to help you meet your goals when you want to start the business or buy the car, understanding the time value of money helps you calculate how much money needs to be put away and for what amount of time.

Often, to understand the time value of money, it is important to be familiar with compound interest. Compound interest involves using formulas that allow the monetary amount of a loan or savings account that earns interest to be calculated. These formulas take into account the principle amount, which is your initial amount, as well as how often the account compounds and the interest rate on the account. For example, if $500 is in a savings account that has a 1% interest rate that compounds twice each year, the amount is going to be $505 after the first six months. Then, the $505 continues earning interest. It does not go back to the principle amount of $500.

Attribution Theory

The attribution theory may also be called the 'explanation theory' or 'cause theory'. Its ideas are built around explaining the reason why something happened. The attribution theory is useful because it helps establish cause-and-effect, however, it can be flawed in the same way. It is not uncommon for people to take credit for positive results while placing external blame when the results are poor.

For example, imagine that a company hires a web designer to redesign their home page in the hopes of attracting new web traffic. If the site experiences more visits over the next few days, the web designer is more likely to attribute it internally, meaning they take credit for the webpage design and its brilliance. However, if the new web page design did not take off or produce results immediately, the designer is more likely to externally attribute or place blame. They might blame the limited amount of time or resources that they had to work on the project.

Two elements of mental model attribution include stable or unstable causes and controllable or uncontrollable causes. A stable cause is one that is consistent. For example, if the person hiring the webpage design gave poor direction, then the cause was stable. If the webpage was designed poorly because the designer did not have much time and did not get enough sleep, it is an unstable cause. Finally, control describes how much control a person has over the situation. If the webpage designer did not like the position, he could have controlled the scenario by choosing a project with a better boss. However, the webpage designer may not have had a choice in who they were designed to, which would make that an uncontrollable factor.

Utilizing Attribution Theory

The attribution theory is among those credited by Charlie Munger as being hugely important to the world of business. The key is taking away personal bias and having a way to clearly view the situation before drawing any conclusions. Once an accurate depiction of the attribution mental model can be formed, through assigning internal and external blame where it is just, then the model can be used to find a better approach.

For example, if the boss is unhappy with the webpage design, it can be easy for him to blame the designer for being incompetent while the designer might blame unclear instructions or not having enough time to produce a quality page. If the two stop assigning blame, they can come together and produce a better webpage. The designer may start by asking for further clarification as to what the boss expects while the boss has an opportunity to re-evaluate their strategy for the homepage and make clarifications. In a case where the web designer blames the external attribution of not having enough time, the pair might come together and agree to a different deadline to minimize the opportunity for the designer to make an excuse. If the webpage were to fail again, then they could not blame the amount of time given, and the plans can be readjusted.

Mean

Mean is commonly used in statistics. It is also referred to as an average that is generally calculated by taking the sum of a group of numbers and then dividing by the number of values that were added together. This is useful when trying to make decisions because it allows you to compare averages and make decisions.

Using Mean as a Mental Model
Imagine that a small start-up was trying to decide if they could afford to hire another employee. Before making this decision, they might try to calculate the average of other salaries and use this to decide if there were enough surplus funds to hire another employee.

The one problem that exists when using averages is that there can be outliers in the data. Using the example with salaries, if the CEO makes a salary of $200,000 yearly and the next highest-earning employee makes $50,000 annually, it is not going to be a fair (or accurate) representation of the dataset and they would not be able to use the average. Sometimes, the outlying data (in this case the CEO's salary) might be excluded to help reach a decision.

Standard Deviation and Normal Distribution

This is commonly used in statistics. The deviation in statistics gives information on how far data points are from each other. Large standard deviations have a diverse data set while small standard deviations are likely to have values that are bunched together. Often, this number is referred to as the 'mean of the mean'. This ties into the mean because the mean is more accurate when the numbers are bunched close together.

Using Standard Deviation as a Mental Model
Standard deviation can also be used to help identify problems. For example, imagine that a company wanted to work to improve customer service. They began surveying customers and plotted their general satisfaction on a graph with the central number being a representation of a perfect experience. By plotting the general level of satisfaction, the company can see how often they are falling short and then make corrections to the process.

Backup Systems

This mental model comes from an engineering framework. There are some critical systems that must work. If they do not, the whole system will fail. A backup system is used to keep the system running even when a critical part fails. This practice may also be called redundancy. Even though something that is redundant is often considered unnecessary, it does not mean that it cannot serve its purpose in the event of a failure. For example, even something as simple as carrying a spare tire in your car can be considered a backup system, as it is something put in place if your tire were to fail in some way.

Using the Backup Systems Mental Model
Essentially, the backup systems mental model describes the importance of having a backup plan should something fail. In engineering, it is common practice to put a backup power system and controls in an airplane, as a failure in an airplane can cause critical problems. In investing, a backup system might be the way investors pick and choose different companies for their portfolio, relying on several means of increasing their income instead of putting all their eggs in one basket.

The major benefit of a backup system is that it prevents that critical period of downtime between a systems failure of some kind and fixing that systems failure. However, not all things need a backup system. To best apply this mental model, consider the consequences of a systems failure. What is going to happen if part of the system breaks? Then, consider the cost of adding a failsafe and if that cost is too much compared to the initial investment. It makes sense to keep a spare tire on hand—the cost of a spare is much less than the cost of your time as you wait for help or the cost of a tow truck.

Breakpoints

Breakpoints are another engineering mental model, this time based on over analysis. It is possible to be too thorough when analyzing information. Think of it this way—with more factors to consider, there is a greater chance of a poor outcome. Likewise, unless you are consistently making the 'right' decision, then there is a greater risk of a poor outcome with every additional decision that you make.

Using the Breakpoint Mental Model
The key to applying the breakpoint mental model is simplicity. Rather than over-complicating decisions or coming up with elaborate, multi-step plans, try to solve problems as simply as possible. With fewer options at your disposal, you're less likely to choose poorly and undo any progress that has been made.

In the world of finance, this can be applied to the over-analysis of information. People who are new to the stock market might focus heavily on making fast, informed decisions and reap short-term benefits. However, these short-term benefits are not as significant as potential long-term gains. Additionally, as short-term profits require constant decision-making when investing, there is a greater chance of making a poor decision and losing the investment.

The Theory of Equilibrium

Though the theory of equilibrium describes a mental model based in the realm of physics, it applies to the idea of balance across the universe. In economics, this equilibrium principle is represented by the idea of supply and demand and the balance across the market. This same principle applies to other areas of life as well. Every action has an equal and opposite reaction. When you can predict these reactions using a mental model, it allows you greater control over what happens next when you are making decisions.

Using the Theory of Equilibrium

In addition to describing reactions and balance, the theory of equilibrium mental model can also be used to describe feedback loops. Feedback loops are world systems that interact. These loops exist in businesses, ecosystems, animals, machines, and other areas. Feedback loops can be positive or negative, with positive representing amplified system output and negative feedback resulting in dampened output. It is important to have a balance of positive and negative feedback loops to create a point of equilibrium. This point of equilibrium is often the solution.

For example, football players suffered many head and neck injuries in the 1950s when players wore leather helmets. Designers worked to create a better helmet, this one being made of plastic and having internal padding. Even though this was better than the leather helmet, it created a positive feedback loop and increased head and neck injuries because the players changed their playing style because they relied more on the protection of the helmet. There was more risk involved with the game because of the positive feedback loop. After a redesign, helmet shells were harder and had better padding, which had the desired outcome of reducing head and neck injuries.

Critical Mass

The critical mass mental model doesn't necessarily have to do with physics, but it is based on principles in physics. In nuclear physics, the critical mass represents the minimum amount of material needed to create an explosion. The materials needed should create a self-sustaining fission reaction.

Likewise, this same principle can be applied to changes in the general thinking of the masses. People's attitudes are hard to change, especially those beliefs that are held by society as a whole. However, as new ideas are presented, developed, and slowly accepted, they gain more momentum, and eventually, that idea reaches the critical mass that is necessary for change.

Using the Critical Mass Mental Model
The critical mass mental model can be applied to any situation that requires a shift that happens over time, or that requires many factors. For example, if a

company decides to implement a new IT system, they will have several steps to ensure that employees can run the new system and it operates smoothly. Without each step, the company can lose money or have problems with data.

This same idea may also be applied to distribution. When the Coca-Cola Company was new, one of the things that set them apart from competitors was their distribution system. With all the resources they had, they were able to reduce overall costs of distribution and pass these savings onto customers, which gave the company a competitive advantage of lesser soda companies of the time.

The Stock Pari-Mutuel System

This mental model was initially developed as a means of gambling on horses. The goal when betting on horses is to only bet when the odds of a certain horse are mispriced. This allows the gambler to take advantage of the situation because there will be a greater payoff if that horse wins. In addition to the current odds for the horses, the gambler must also study the performance of the horses in different races.

Using the Stock Pari-Mutuel System
This mental model has several applications when decision-making, as it speaks to the importance of knowing when to take risks. Ultimately, people who are successful in life do not always make the safest

choice. Jeff Bezos would not have created Amazon had he not been willing to take the risk. Investors like Warren Buffett and Charlie Munger would not be as successful without taking some risk, as it is impossible to make the right decisions all the time.

When taking risks, it is a lot like betting on a horse. It is important to take risks only when the potential payoff outweighs any potential risk. Likewise, one should only take risks when there is a higher chance of a favorable outcome. It would do a gambler little good to bet on a horse that has placed second-to-last in 8/10 of the last races even if the payoff would be great because it is unlikely the horse is going to perform well.

Mental Models in Economics

Economics requires a different type of thought than physics and other subjects. Generally, it is the study of how people make decisions based on their available money, including buying and saving habits relative to their salary. By understanding the general demographic of a group, prices can be set for goods that fulfill supply and demand. In addition to economics affecting sales, economists might study issues across the field of economy to identify problems. Among the key principles in economics that is useful to understand include:

- Law of Supply and Demand- This law describes the inverse relationship between the quality of a good and the price. Factors like the availability of a good (and its substitutes), the overall cost of the good, ad the economic standing of the buyer all affect demand. This law goes on to further describe the positive relationship that exists between the quantity of a good and its price. The cost of materials and other inputs, technological costs, and overall price all affect the number of goods supplied to the public.

- Income and Substitution Effects- Substitutes are goods that consumers buy instead of a similar product that has increased in price. When the price of something falls, the substitution effect describes the way that a consumer has more purchasing power, being able to buy the same product with less money. The income effect describes a consumer's tendency to use more of a good that drops in price because it is more available.

- Utility & Rationality- The average consumer behaves rationally when purchasing, trying to use goods to their full extent. By choosing goods they can use, it increases general happiness with purchasing that product.

- Scarcity- This principle describes people's attitude when there are few goods and higher demand. When an item is scarce, people are willing to pay more for what is considered a limited opportunity they may miss out on.

- Elasticity- The elasticity of a variable is how sensitively it reacts to another variable. For example, changes in overall income may affect supply and demand, which also affects the overall price of certain goods. Put simply, elasticity measures responsiveness. Some necessary goods like water may be inelastic since the supply and demand do not change as price increases or decreases—people still need water.

- Monopolization- Gas stations that are in the middle of rural areas are an example of monopolies, as they can inflate the cost of gas as much as they would like because people in the area still need gas and only have that company as an option. This happens when there is no similar substitute, and a customer is forced to pay an inflated price for a good or service.

- Oligopolies- Ogliopolies compete against companies offering similar goods or services through the quality of the product or service or advertising. They may also significantly reduce prices, though this can cause others to reduce prices as well and cause a significant reduction across the board. One of the problems with oligopolies is that it is harder for new corporations to enter the market, as they do not have the same resources for competing that more established companies likely have.

Using the Principles of Economics as a Mental Model
As you put together these many principles, it begins to create a framework for understanding economics. As economics has many moving parts, it is important to understand all these areas to be successful in areas like finance, business ownership, and marketing.

Pavlovian Conditioning

Understanding condition mental models are essential to understanding motivation and the way that the human mind makes connections between different ideas. Conditioning brings about an instant response that is the result of responding to certain stimuli. These responses are programmed, either through consciously creating relationships between a behavioral action and an event or by this relationship forming naturally over time. There are three types of conditioning; classic, operant, and instrumental conditioning.

Classical conditioning refers to stimuli that cause an emotional response. For example, someone whose grandmother baked may remember the smell of chocolate chip cookies from their childhood and any time they smell chocolate chip cookies they are reminded of their grandmother. This same principle can also be used in marketing. For example, the Coca

Cola Company often has upbeat, enjoyable commercials that help people make the association between positive feelings and drinking Coca Cola.

Instrumental conditioning relies on positive or negative reinforcement to either continue or discontinue a behavior. For example, when trademarks are associated with a positive image, prospective customers are more likely to choose to do business with them. Another concept in sales is the sale of a product that is priced higher than comparable items. As higher-priced items are considered higher quality, people may be more likely to but the expensive item than the inexpensive ones.

Finally, operant conditioning describes associative learning. Essentially, a reward is used to encourage the behavior. The most famous experiments were carried out by Frederick Skinner. Skinner trained pigeons and rats to press a lever. They learned this behavior and would receive a food reward, so they were more likely to repeat it.

Using Conditioning as a Mental Model
Conditioning is used best as a general influence strategy. When we want people to like things, we create an association between that item and a positive emotion or experience. Likewise, when we want someone to turn away from something or see it in a negative light, it should be associated with negative emotions or connotations. For example, it is not

uncommon for commercials promoting a vegetarian lifestyle to show firsthand what the meat industry is like and the suffering of animals. It is their hope that the negative feelings this inspires encourages more people to reduce their meat consumption.

Another way this can be used is to identify people's motives. Often, people react in a certain way because they are either positively or negatively influenced by certain stimuli.

The Why Model

When trying to influence, one of the most important things that an authority can ask is 'why'. It is impossible to convince someone to change their opinion on something without a reason why. This why serves as a predecessor of justification. It clarifies a person's reasoning and prepares someone to take action.

Using the Why Mental Model

The Why mental model is one of the easiest constructs to master. First, you clarify your reasoning or justification by understanding why yourself. As you access this information, your intentions become clearer and it becomes easier to solve problems and make decisions that align with your attentions.

Another benefit of the why model is that it allows you to tap into the 'why' of other people's minds as well. It can help you clarify people's intentions when communicating ideas or understand what customers need. By understanding the reasoning behind actions, you can choose your words in a way that represents those needs.

Why makes ideas and actions mean something. It is the purpose behind everything. When why is asked, and an idea is broken down completely, it clarifies a path of action that can be taken.

Entropy

The entropy mental model is a tricky one, as it is used across many different disciplines and may have slightly different meanings in each one. It exists in cosmology, thermodynamics, statistical mechanics, information theory, and ore. Put simply, entropy represents the randomness that exists within a system. When entropy is high, so is the likelihood of randomness. When randomness is high, that makes it harder to predict an outcome with a high degree of certainty.

Using Entropy as a Mental Model
The best way to use entropy is to remember that there are things you will not be able to control in life. Even though it is ideal to always have favorable outcomes, life rarely works that way. As you try to control things outside of your power, it often results in disappointment and ultimately failure.

Rather than obsessing over things you cannot control, work toward solving problems and learning what you can control. Once you know what is within the scope of your control, you'll no longer feel powerless in your life. Additionally, you will do away with the unhealthy fixation on things that occur outside the scope of your control.

Inversion

We touched on the idea of inversion briefly already. Put simply, this means working through a problem backward. Inversion is often used because it is a better strategy for deconstructing and understanding a problem in its entirety. It also can help you more grounded and calm, as it gives you the opportunity to reflect on the ultimate consequences of any action you may choose.

Using the Inversion Mental Model
Let's look at a common example for a business owner. Imagine that a small business owner wanted to increase revenue by 50% of the second year of operation. They plan aggressively to try and meet this goal, making ambitious assumptions and projects for the company. Often, these initial ambitions fail because they are too ambitious and unrealistic. Instead of working through the problem forward and deciding how much will be projected for revenue each quarter, it is better to work through the problem backward. Smaller actions can be taken that ensure a

company's financial longevity and prevent bankruptcy. Once a level of security is added, the business can use their additional resources to make bolder decisions that are more likely to result in the revenue that they are projecting.

The inversion mental model can also be used to consider the consequences of an action. Even if you only have a 15% chance of succeeding, simply by identifying that small chance, you help yourself reach a grounded state. This grounded state allows calm, rational thought that will be more likely to achieve success. As you identify parameters of success, it also reduces the chance of failure because you become more confident in your ability to handle the obstacles in your way.

Autocatalysis

This is a principle of chemistry that can be applied to anything that is considered 'self-breeding'. Chemistry is based on interactions. An autocatalysis speeds up a process or reaction, creating a level of stability that gives the reaction time to stabilize and then jump to the next part of the process. In most cases, the catalyst itself is not directly involved in the reaction, and it is not influenced by the process. For example, a couple getting married needs an official to move to the next part of the process. Once the marriage has been officiated, the official does not participate in the other parts of the wedding, and the official is unaffected. The official is the catalyst in this case, as he or she can go on to officiate other weddings (be a part of other reactions).

Using the Autocatalysis Mental Model
The autocatalysis mental model explains things that are self-started as well. These act as their own catalyst and result in positive outcomes. For example, Disney had already created several movies by the time the video cassette tape came out. Even though they were already popular, they were limited by the availability of film in the average home. Once video cassettes were available, they only had to take what they already owned the copyright to (the Disney movies) and put them on tape. In this way, Disney spurred its own success.

Natural Selection

Natural selection is a biological framework that describes the adaptation of a species and how species change based on their environment. The earliest ideas of natural selection were presented by Charles Darwin, who studied the various animals across the Galapagos Islands. Darwin found that the different species of birds, tortoises, and other animals were similar but different, with each having unique features that allowed it to eat, find shelter, and survive in the specific environment of its native island.

This applies even to human society today, as the people who are most successful are generally those who are best adapted to change. By accepting change and learning how to embrace it, a person gains power over their experience. They can take that change and transform it in a way that it is productive.

Using the Natural Selection Mental Model
The natural selection mental model can be used to explain any type of adaptation. For example, if a company discovers a new way to produce something that is more affordable than the process used by competitors, they can produce the same item and generate higher revenue. In your personal life, this can be applied to the idea of adapting to your environment. People often get comfortable where they are. While there is nothing wrong with feeling safe or content, this contentedness will not last forever, and there is no growth that can be experienced without change. Embracing the law of natural selection also means embracing changes in your life and learning how to make them work for you, rather than succumbing to whatever obstacles you face.

Pareto's Principle

Pareto's Principle was established by Italian economist Vilfredo Pareto in the early 1900s as he searched for a formula that described the unequal distribution of wealth across Italy. According to Pareto's observations, 20% of the people in Italy owned 80% of the nation's wealth. Oddly, this formula would apply to much more than just unequal wealth distribution.

Today, the expanded definition of Pareto's principle is an equation that explains economic inequality. It has been tested in many areas. For example, research shows about 20% of the posts on a blog are responsible for 80% of the site's traffic. Additionally, 80% of a company's total revenue comes from 20% of its customers. There are examples of this all across economics.

Applying Pareto's Principle as a Mental Model
When applying Pareto's principle to your personal life or work, you can significantly improve your productivity. Here are a few tips:

- Look at your to-do list. Instead of focusing on all the small tasks, choose about 20% of the tasks that make up 80% of the results. By turning your attention to these items first, you can prioritize your day and maximize what you are able to get done.
- In marketing, focus on those customers that generate the most revenue. Invest time and money in identifying, understanding, and seeking similar customers and target them.
- When assessing risks, focus on those risks with greater significance. In most cases, not everything is going to go wrong. Those areas

that have the highest potential for damage should be focused on, while the rest are minimized. Do not avoid them altogether if they become an issue, just be sure to distribute your efforts as needed.

- Identify quality issues if 20% of products are responsible for 80% of complaints. By going straight to the issue, products can be re-evaluated and better strategies can be introduced.

- Know what goals are most important. It can be easy to be ambitious and put too much on your plate. However, as you evaluate goals, know which ones are most significant and will produce the best results. Not all goals are created equally.

Another way to look at Pareto's Principle is for guidance when making decisions. There is a small number of variables (20%) that affect 80% of the outcome when decision-making. By identifying these few variables that are important instead of focusing on too many small factors, a person can improve their chance of a positive outcome and clarify their thought processes.

Cumulative Advantage

Also called 'The Matthew Effect', this law simply means that people who are rich get richer and people who are poor get poorer. For example, this may happen when the most senior member at a law firm is awarded a high profile case. Even though there are likely other qualified lawyers at the firm, they were not given the opportunity because the 'richer' (more experienced) lawyer was awarded the prize. This granted him more experienced, as well.

Another example is the board game 'Monopoly'. At the beginning of the game, all players use the same dice to roll for their turns. They are presented with the same board and the same resources (money). Therefore, they have more opportunity. As the game unfolds, however, opportune investments by some players on key pieces of property give them the upper hand. As they become richer and their opponents become poorer, they continue to rise in their riches until they monopolize the entire board and win the game. As a player becomes more advantaged, they have additional resources (properties) to collect more money and are less likely to land on other players' properties.

Applying the Cumulative Advantage Mental Model
The work world can be a competitive place. The best way to have a cumulative advantage is to build one. Choose a career that you can grow with instead of remaining stagnant. When you have the opportunity, build your wealth instead of letting it sit. Make investments that will increase your cumulative

advantage. By doing these things, you increase your likelihood of success.

Removal/Avoidance of Harm

Also known as *via negativa,* this mental model involves omitting those things that are harmful or bad. Many people overlook the benefits of omitting things in favor of adding something new. For example, some doctors might try to treat cancer using medication instead of removing it because they try to do whatever is going to cause the least amount of harm. As medication is less invasive, it is often the go-to for cancer treatment.

It is not always enough to add good elements, however. For example, a company that has poor shipping practices might have great products. As customers are not happy with the way their products are being delivered, however, they lose business regardless of the quality of their products.

Applying Avoidance of Harm as a Mental Model
When you are gathering information on a problem or scenario, try to remove the bad elements before adding good ones. Often, it does not matter how many 'good' elements are added if the bad one is acting as the weakest link. Think of it this way—you wouldn't punish a whole group of children if one child is going around bullying everyone. It is much more effective to remove the problem child.

Multiplying by Zero

It does not matter what number you multiply by zero—the result will always be nothing. Even though this is a basic math principle, it can also be applied to a simple principle—a system is only as strong as its weakest link. For example, imagine that a group of five men was captured by an enemy that wanted to know the location of a weapon. The group of men is only as strong as the weakest one because if even one of them gives up the information, the others cannot stop it from happening.

Applying the Multiplicative System Mental Model
The multiplicative system is only as strong as the weakest link, however, an additive system lets all the components come and work together. An additive system is like a Thanksgiving dinner. Adding time spent with family with ingredients like a turkey, stuffing, potatoes, yams, green bean casserole, and cranberry sauce adds to the function as a whole. If the green bean casserole is burnt, it takes away from the whole slightly but not as much because there are so many elements. If someone brings dessert, then this adds to the scenario, but not that much.

In business, it is not uncommon for companies to believe they are operating in an additive system even though they are operating in a multiplicative one. For example, companies may add new products continuously but have horrible customer service. Even though they have a variety of new products, because they have failed at customer service, they may have many customers that refuse to come back. Therefore, they cannot sell their new products and they do not add to the equation at all.

In your life, it is important to focus on running on an additive system. Be aware of weak links. When you notice something adding up to zero in your system, work to improve in that area instead of focusing on adding more to your life with other ones.

Incentives

Incentives are at the heart of many people's decision-making and behaviors. For example, someone who goes to rehab and gets clean may stay that way for several months until their partner splits up with them. If they had chosen to get clean because of their partner, then they will likely relapse because they no longer have that incentive in front of them.

Behavioral changes are not usually brought on by reasoning with a person. They need a greater incentive than words to help them change their behavior. Some of the most famous work on incentives was carried out by B.F. Skinner. He focused on those behaviors that he could observe rather than questioning what was happening in a person's or animal's head.

Teaching new behaviors works best with positive reinforcement. Continuous reinforcement describes the reinforcement of a behavior every time it is exhibited. This works well when training a dog a new trick, however, the reward needs to be instant for the dog to make the association. Intermittent reinforcement is done on a schedule. This is a good way of maintaining behaviors that a subject has already learned. For example, a recovering alcoholic may be reminded of their success intermittently when they receive chips for being sober for a certain amount of months or years.

In business, intermittent reinforcement is most commonly used. For example, employees might be encouraged to be more productive by being offered a bonus for assembling a certain number of parts. However, it does not make sense to pay the employees each time they complete a part—it would be uneconomical and inefficient. Instead, the payment would be received intermittently as part of their regular check.

Scheduled reinforcement in the business world often involves payment on a different schedule. Sometimes, bonuses are offered for additional work. Fixed-ratio schedules describe payments based on the work completed. Freelance contractors are usually paid per project that they complete. This has a high response to reinforcement, as there is no payment if the work does not get completed.

Variable-ratio schedules have varying amounts and numbers of reinforcements. These schedules are unpredictable—people like gamblers, salespeople, and telemarketers may be paid on this schedule. This is still effective—Skinner observed a hungry pigeon peck a disk 12,000 times, offering the positive reinforcement of food after every 110 pecks.

Finally, fixed-interval schedules are the most common form of payment. They are most commonly used for hourly wages or salaries, where people are paid based on the amount of time spent on a specific task. This has the lowest response rate, and employees are not generally as motivated by this form of payment.

According to work done by Skinner, the least effective way to change behavior is punishment. Unless a punishment is consistently present, the behavior is likely to reoccur whenever the punishment is not immediately administered. For example, an employee may not use social media when their boss is around, but they may be on social media when they are left unattended. The threat is gone, so they are no longer worried about the punishment. Another problem is that punishment can trigger the fight-or-flight response. This can cause a link between punishment and aggression, which explains the trend of abusive parents coming from abusive families. The final issue is that punishment causes many things, including feelings of escape, aggression, and helplessness. What it does not cause, however, is a desire to learn new and better responses. The mind has barriers when it is in this state, and it is almost impossible to learn a new behavior. Punishment also fails to teach new behaviors, making it ineffective because it only teaches what not to do.

Applying Incentives as a Mental Model
When you understand the incentives that align with a person's core beliefs, you gain insight into how these incentives might influence their thoughts and actions. By understanding incentives, it becomes possible to create a win-win scenario, where every party involved benefits.

For example, Joe Wilson visited the Xerox company after the sales of the new, better machine were lower than the sales of the older, less-sophisticated machine. The salesmen were being given a commission to sell the older model, so they had pushed that on customers instead.

This mental model can be used to create working relationships, both personal relationships, and work relationships.

Complex Adaptive Systems

One of the best examples of a complex adaptive system is a car. Cars have many parts that must all work together to keep the vehicle running. The car cannot run if the starter is broken or the timing belt is loose. All these pieces must interact for the car to move in a functional way.

This can also be applied to traffic. If there is a car accident, and there are rescue vehicles on the side of the road, people may slow down and look over as they pass the area. As they slow down, the people behind them slow down. This goes back, so on and so forth, and eventually, there is a traffic jam that has come from the interaction of all the parts of the system.

This also happens in places like the stock market. The stock market is a complex system of investors, all of them buying and selling stocks for various entities. Forecasting can be challenging, as the people within the system are constantly adapting their behavior based on how the market is moving around. This can get confusing, as the state of the market can fluctuate several points every day.

However, each of these cogs in the stock market affects the others. For example, a market forecaster might successfully predict that the market is going to crash. He is right. The forecaster makes the same prediction several years later, and everyone believes him, promoting the quick sale of stocks and a crash, simply because the forecaster caused a panic.

Applying Complex Advanced Systems as a Mental Model

Complex advanced systems have many moving parts. These moving parts each have an effect on the whole, setting a chain reaction in motion. When looking at a complex system, it is important not to jump to conclusions or make assumptions about the cause-and-effect. With more moving parts, there is a lower likelihood of being able to see the full picture and identify the cause. Instead, tackle these problems by looking at the beginning and the end, analyzing risk, reward, and probability, and then choosing a course of action.

Leverage

Leverage is an idea that has been explored for centuries. It is believed the ancient Egyptians must have been familiar with this practice, using levers to lift large stones weight as much as 100 tons while building the obelisks and pyramids of Egypt. Even though it is a physical principle, it can also be applied to thought. Leverage describes a small kernel of information or common ground that can be used to help someone negotiate or make a point.

Think of it this way:

"You don't convince people by challenging their longest and most firmly held opinions. You find common ground and work from there. Or you look for leverage to make them listen. Or you create an alternative with so much support from other people that the opposition voluntarily abandons its views and joins your camp."

-Ryan Holiday

People are naturally resistant to ideas that do not align with their core beliefs and values. Additionally, it is nearly impossible to change these without first having an 'in'. That 'in' is information about their background that might help you interest them in your cause or something that unites you on common ground, showing that you have similar beliefs in other areas. Once you have this leverage, it becomes easier to persuade and negotiate.

Applying Leverage as a Mental Model
As a mental model, leverage refers to small, well-focused actions. These actions should produce significant improvements or results when applied in the right place. For example, a person may try to lose weight by drinking smoothies instead of a meal once per day. This increase in fruits and vegetables can improve digestive health and boost weight loss. However, the smoothie is best enjoyed in the morning or at lunch. If a person were to drink a sugary smoothie before bed, the calories would likely hang out around their middle and hinder their efforts to lose weight.

Leverage can also be applied to business and negotiations. Anything can be leverage. Imagine that you take your car into the repair shop, estimating that you have a bad wheel bearing. After an estimate for the bearing at $80, you bring the car in and leave. When you pick the car up the next day, the auto repairman states that there are several other problems that will cost hundreds to fix. As you do not know anything about cars, you cannot necessarily disprove him. You may feel stuck or obligated to let him make the repairs he claims. In this case, the auto repairman is more knowledgeable, so he has the leverage.

This happens when negotiating prices in business too. For example, movie snacks are often over-priced because people are not allowed to bring outside food and drinks into the movies. Music sites like Youtube, Pandora, and Spotify are free to use because the free versions come with advertisements and the companies can make money from advertising fees.

To establish leverage yourself, it is important to remember that leverage is based on perception. It only works if one party believes the other has an advantage. Additionally, as new information becomes available, the amount of leverage can change. For example, your auto repairman may say something different if you tell him thank you for replacing the wheel bearing and go to get a second opinion on the other repairs he recommended. The leverage also ceases to exist if one party decides to exit the relationship. Finally, remember that leverage is situation-specific. Even though you might not have leverage at the auto mechanic shop, you may have leverage at work or with clients.

Velocity

Velocity and speed are two different things. Speed measures the distance that is traveled over time. It has little to do with spatial awareness—a person could run miles around the same small circle, and they still wouldn't be moving anywhere. Velocity, on the other hand, measures a person's displacement or the amount they have moved from their previous location. Therefore, it is velocity and not speed that we want to use to make our choices in life.

Applying Velocity as a Mental Model

Velocity is direction-aware, whereas speed occurs one-dimensionally. The people who grow the most are those with great velocity who think multi-dimensionally. You can apply this to your life by choosing how and where you allocate your efforts. You can spend your time speeding around and getting nowhere or you can choose to put forth your efforts in a way that is going to push you forward toward your goals.

In the workplace, you can increase velocity by shaving away unnecessary tasks. While you'll need to do the minimum requirements for your job, it is not necessary to attend every single non-mandatory meeting or carry out unnecessary tasks. Get in the habit of saying 'no'. Even though saying 'yes' is a great way to be introduced to opportunity, saying 'yes' too often can leave you doing tasks for everyone else and unfocused on your own velocity.

In addition to knowing when to say 'yes', try to chunk time better. When you can sit down and focus on one task at a time, it gives you a greater chance of productivity. By increasing your productivity, you end up with more time for the tasks that matter.

Activation Energy

Activation energy describes the amount of energy needed to kickstart a chemical reaction. For example, if you are lighting a log on fire, a match is not going to be enough, but a flamethrower is going to be excessive. The activation energy is the barrier that exists between these values, being the smallest amount of reactants and products that will create the chemical reaction.

Applying Activation Energy as a Mental Model
Understanding activation energy helps us control our surroundings. For example, a book is made of paper, which is flammable. However, it is not considered a

fire hazard if it is sitting alone on a stand, because there is no fire nearby that could act as activation energy. If a candle is set next to the book on the stand, however, it is best to move the book away to prevent the fire. In a way, activation energy makes the world a safer place because it places limits on chemical reactions.

Even change requires activation energy. When you are trying to bring about new things in your life, you must embrace change. For example, if you are unhappy in your job, the most logical step is to see what else is out there. You have many options—taking a night class to learn a new skill, finding a new job, or specializing in a different area altogether. Before you can do any of these things, however, you may have to register or put out applications or do something else that sparks that activation energy necessary for change.

Cooperation

Many biological systems are competitive. Humans compete for resources and wealth, while animals compete for food, shelter, and other resources. Even so, there are many times when cooperation becomes a useful, if not a necessary part of the biological process.

Without cooperation, it would be impossible for any one group to survive. For example, bacteria and the first simple-celled organism had to come together to create a complex cellular being. There are many symbiotic relationships like this in the animal kingdom. For example, pilot fish often swim around with the protection of sharks. The sharks do not eat them because the pilot fish clean the sharks' teeth.

This is also seen in game theory in the Prisoner's Dilemma. In this scenario, two prisoners are said to be better off if they cooperate. If one of them is cheating, however, it is better if the second is cheating as well. This makes it hard for them to cooperate, especially if they do not trust each other.

Using Cooperation as a Mental Model
Cooperation is important for developing relationships that are mutually beneficial. Even though the Prisoner's Dilemma presents a complicated scenario, cooperation is almost always possible in the real world. The goal when cooperating should always be to reach a decision that is satisfying for both parties. By identifying another person's wants/needs and knowing your own wants/needs, it becomes possible to reach a solution that benefits all parties involved.

Hierarchical Instincts

Many complex organisms live within a hierarchy. In bee and ant colonies, each insect is assigned a job based on their gender. The queen bee or queen ant is at the top of the hierarchy. In a pride, a lion is at the top of a hierarchy, and others follow him. Even humans exist within a hierarchy, as we have a source of authority that tells us as a society how to act and behave.

This need for a hierarchy comes from the need to look to a leader, especially in times of stress. One famous set of experiments was the Milgram experiments that showed the human bias toward authoritative figures. In the experiment, the 'teacher' asked the 'learner' questions. When the question was answered incorrectly, a shock was administered. The shocks increased to high levels, some which would have been fatal if the experiments had been real.

The participants of the study were instructed to give the shock at the command of the teacher. Many of them obeyed, despite banging and audible protests from the 'learner'. When they felt uncomfortable, verbal prods were given that insisted the participant continue administering the shocks. The teachers told them that they 'must go on' or 'continue'. Many continued giving the shock despite protests, up until the learner fell silent after the final shock was administered.

Using Hierarchical Instincts as a Mental Model
It is human nature to obey authority. We may feel obligated to say 'yes' when our boss or spouse asks us to do something. However, this can be detrimental if the tasks being assigned to you are preventing you from focusing on those things you need to do.

Something else to remember is that even experts can be incorrect or biased. If you have doubts, do your own research and do not take someone's word for it. Even though it is healthy to have respect for authority, do not let that level of respect overshadow your ability to think for yourself. You are still responsible for your own actions and ultimately the ethics that you choose to conduct your life with.

Milgram's experiments were carried out after the events of Nazi Germany to test the ideas of authority and how it influenced a person's behavior. Many soldiers reported they were blindly following orders, as they were instructed to. In Milgram's first experiments, all people administered at least 300 volts of electricity despite their resistance in doing so. Some were physically uncomfortable, biting their lips, sweating, stuttering, trembling, and digging their fingernails into their skin. Twenty-six of forty or 65% of participants went on to administer the shock of 450-volts. It becomes clear that even when it seems like authority may be doing something unethical, it is hard for the average person to speak up.

Parkinson's Law

This law states that the amount of time assigned to a project is the amount of time that project is going to take. For example, an employee may be given three hours to update the company's financial records, a task that might take 60-90 minutes usually. Even though they have more time allotted than they would normally, they find themselves procrastinating and distracted. In the final 45 minutes are so, they will be panicking, trying to rush through the tasks that could have been completed much sooner.

Using Parkinson's Law as a Mental Model
Parkinson's Law can be most beneficially applied to your day-to-day activities at work. Instead of giving yourself large chunks of time to complete assignments, break them down into smaller parts. For example, if you have a week to complete a project, break it down into smaller milestones and assign them to different days. If you follow the deadlines you have set for yourself, you end up finishing on time and without sacrificing sleep the night before the deadline.

The Butterfly Effect

Many science fiction movies have discussed the phenomena known as the Butterfly Effect, an occurrence where a small, insignificant action has a big impact. In one movie from the 1960s, a butterfly flapped its wings, and its non-linear effects caused a typhoon. This idea is also common in time travel movies—changing something in the past nearly always alters the future in some unforeseeable way. Of course, even if butterflies don't usually cause typhoons, this is representative of the idea that small events can act as their own catalysts and have large, grandiose results.

Applying the Butterfly Effect as a Mental Model

Mental models represent a complex system. Unfortunately, the small details (like a butterfly flapping its wings) can be overlooked because it is impossible to know if the non-linear effects are going to be minuscule or catastrophic. When you are making decisions or solving problems using mental models, it is important to remember that you cannot possibly account for every small detail. Otherwise, there would be so many factors that there would be a higher risk of an unknown outcome, and the system would become overcomplicated rather than simplifying things.

This same idea can be seen in economics. The economy is incredibly complex, especially with the development of better communication technology and the globalization of many products and services. Of course, this also means that there is a greater interconnectedness than ever before. Like with a butterfly, some events in economics can have a compounding impact of small changes. Even one area of the market being volatile can cause catastrophic declines in economic health.

The Tragedy of the Commons

The Tragedy of the Commons describes an illustration of the depletion of common resources. For example, imagine that a large area of land was home to many cows that could feed and roam freely. The area was commonly shared by many herdsmen and they could take cattle as needed for food. However, as the herdsmen consider the potential for achieving better social status, they ponder the idea of taking a cow for their own herd and then selling it. Now, the focus is not on sharing the common area, but on maximizing the herdsman's own gain.

The problem is that this behavior is likely to be mimicked by the other herdsmen as well. They may continue to seek gain and add to their herd limitlessly—until the limits are reached and the land has been significantly depleted.

This happens because men, like all creatures, are self-preserving. Rather than focusing on what is best for the entirety of mankind, they pursue what is best for themselves and their own survival.

Using the Tragedy of the Common as a Mental Model
The Tragedy of the Common insists on the division of resources. Without this division, man is likely to act in their own best interest. Consider the devastating effects that runoff from agricultural lands, factories, and waste areas on the land. Pollution is a serious problem in many areas, and the planet is hotter than it has been in years. Even so, large corporations continue to pollute the water, land, and air and take from the natural resources. These are then turned to profit that benefits larger corporations, rather than the average person.

In business, this can also be applied to the division of resources. For example, if the company offers free drinks to their employees through the day, but only spend a set amount of money, the employees that arrive first may take the drinks. If each employee were offered 1-2 drinks daily instead, this would ensure the resources were shared among all the employees and not just those that were looking out for their own best interest.

The Lollapalooza Effect

This final mental model has been saved for last because it describes your personal network. As you build on your knowledge base and become more familiar with the mental models at your disposal, the Lollapalooza Effect starts to take place. Essentially, this happens when various models are combined to produce a certain outcome, usually one that is dramatic. For example, in recent decades, researchers have been searching for a treatment that would suppress and fight the HIV virus. Recently, these efforts were successful when several drugs were combined (instead of using a single drug) to create an extremely effective treatment regimen.

Using the Lollapalooza Effect
The easiest way to use the Lollapalooza Effect is to create connections between the various mental models you understand. Each time you learn a new mental model, take the time to reflect on the other

models you have learned. Think about how this information ties into what you already know and situations where it might apply at work and in your life. By getting in the habit of overlapping your mental models, you'll find yourself better equipped when it is time for problem-solving or decision making.

Chapter 7:

Using Mental Models for Decision Making

One of the most daunting parts of the decision-making process is deciding where to start. How can you possibly determine which mental model to use if you do not have a clear picture of what you are dealing with? This chapter will break down guidelines for using mental models for decision making.

#1: Asking the Right Questions

Asking questions like who, what, when, where, and why can be used to help identify information before you begin working on a mental model. As you answer these questions, you'll require critical insight into the situation that you are dealing with. By asking factual questions like these and giving a direct answer, it provides you with the factual information that is not based on biased or skewed information. Once you have all the who, what, when, where, and why questions figured out, you can move on to the next step.

#2: Considering Potential Problems

One of the reasons that people experience poor outcomes from decision making is because they work through the problem forwards instead of backward. Moving forwards means tackling problems as they arise. The problem is that leaves the person or corporation making the decisions unprepared. Rather than having an idea of what might go wrong and how to potentially fix it, they must spend time researching what exactly is going wrong and how to approach it before coming up with a plan. This costs valuable time that people do not always have.

For example, imagine that somebody wanted to start a florist business. Even though there is the option of growing their own flowers, that might not always produce predictable results, especially if they grow outdoors where they cannot completely control the environment. In addition to considering how they are going to grow and source the flowers, they'll also need a plan for keeping the flowers preserved until they are ordered. With a well-thought-out plan, it is much more likely that the company will experience success. If the florist shop does not take the time to plan out these different steps, they are less likely to know what to do when they need to source more flowers to fulfill orders or if there is a problem with the coolers that they store the flowers in.

#3: Consider the 10-10-10 Principle

Like the regret minimization framework used by Jeff Bezos, the 10-10-10 Principle helps you look at a situation and critically before making decisions. Basically, you consider the decision and how it will make you feel 10 minutes from now, 10 months from now, and 10 years from now. This is a great strategy for evaluating the short-term and long-term benefits of a goal, both in the near and distant future. As you consider the 10-10-10 Principle for each of your possible decisions, you'll find the best course of action that benefits you in the short-term and long-term.

#4: Know What Has the Most Influence

When you are making a decision, some factors have greater weight than others. It is important to know what matters most. Otherwise, you'll spend so much time focusing on unimportant details that it will be hard to see how they fit into the equation and their effect on the outcome. If you can, try to breakdown the parts of your decision into what matters the most. Choose 3-4 areas that are most concerning to you and consider how your decision will affect each.

For example, imagine that someone is considering moving to another state. Their parents live in their current location. If they are really close to their parents, the proximity might be more significant to the decision than it would be for someone who was estranged from their family.

#5: Ask for Outside Perspectives

Even once you begin to remove bias from your thinking and develop mental models in many fields, it is important to remember that every person is an asset with their own perspective. When you are unsure of a decision or your possible options, don't be afraid to ask a friend, coworker, or family member for advice. The only thing that an outside perspective will do is give you a chance to look at your decision in a new way. Sometimes, the is exactly what is needed to make a clear-headed choice.

#6: Study Similar Scenarios

Many people who are successful spend their free time researching various ideas, strategies, and scenarios, how people responded, and the overall outcome. By studying similar scenarios, it becomes possible to learn more and look at things from a new perspective. Additionally, by broadening your research into an area, you increase your expertise. This will help with problem-solving in the future and as you lay a foundation on which you can build more mental models.

#7: Consider Several Options

As you broaden your mental models, you'll find there is a greater range of possibilities at your disposal when decision-making. Doing away with bias and assumptions in your thinking also opens your mind and broadens your perspectives, giving you more options. It is okay to brainstorm ideas and jot down several things. Once you feel satisfied, go through the list and pick out 3-4 that are the most likely to have a good outcome.

As you consider which of your options is most viable, consider the risk, reward, and probability. Once you have chosen at least 3-4 choices, visualize each of them and possible outcomes. Most scenarios have more than one possible outcome, with some outcomes being more likely than others. You can use decision trees to help with this.

Chapter 8:

Using Mental Models for Problem Solving

Solving real-life problems is not always as straightforward as solving a problem in math—there can be more than one answer and there is not always a 'right' solution. The goal, therefore, must be to choose the solution that is going to have the most favorable outcome. Understanding mental models is a critical part of the problem-solving process. It affects the way that we perceive details about a situation, how these details relate to each other in our mind, and the range of solutions that we are capable of coming up with. This chapter will provide some guidelines for using mental models for problem-solving. With these steps, you'll be able to choose the best possible solution with the greatest chance of a positive outcome.

#1: Know Your Specialties

It was mentioned earlier that the people who are most successful are those who have studied in a wide range of disciplines, being able to overlap the principles from their studies and form a latticework of mental models. Even though the eventual goal is to master all these mental models, it is impossible to do all that at once. As you learn, you are building on your knowledge. The best way to do this is to start with a strong foundation.

Even though it can be easy to want to be the person to come up with the solution, our own desire to be 'right' can get in the way of what is most important—solving the problem in the best way possible. Other people have unique strengths and perceptions and allowing them input can help develop a solution that you may have overlooked. Know when you are not necessarily the best person for the job and be open to other perceptions and ideas. This is known as a circle of competence in investing, or an area where a person is most well-educated. By knowing what you do know and what you do not, involve yourself with those situations that can be solved using your unique skill set of mental models.

#2: Be Wary of Bias

When bias clouds your judgment, it becomes impossible to see the full scope of a situation. The problem is that many people are not aware of their own individual bias or the way it affects their perception of the world. One of the best tools to use when problem-solving is to write down only the facts. By focusing on what you know, it stops you from jumping to conclusions and making assumptions.

One of the obstacles in identifying bias is that people experience it in unique ways. It can be hard to pinpoint exactly what is causing your bias or how it is influencing problem-solving. Here are some of the most common kinds of bias:

- Overconfidence bias- People tend to assume they are right. However, this can lead to false optimism about what you know and what you do not know. This can result in erroneous information that makes it hard to truly solve a problem.

- Selective perception- We are all limited to our own worldviews. However, by focusing too much on your own perspective, it can cause you to interpret information based on perception rather than fact. Selective perception is a problem because it takes our focus away from all the elements at hand and turns it to whatever parts of the problem we choose to give our attention to. The alternatives developed are also limited by selective perception. Confirmation bias is another type of selective perception where people ignore information that does not support their current ideas.

- Anchoring bias- This type of bias often refers to first impressions or initial information that we receive on someone. As people generally seek out information that confirms their initial thoughts on something, they do not always adjust appropriately when new information is presented.

- Framing- This type of bias exists for those times when a person allows themselves to be influenced by the way a problem is presented. For example, a company has an Earnings per Share of $1.25. They may frame this by noting the expectations, which were $1.27 or by comparing the earnings to a previous period where they were $1.21. Even though the same information is communicated, it is better to report this amount as being greater than they were in the previous period than to report they were lower than expected for the quarter.

- Availability Bias- Sometimes, people do not necessarily want the most accurate answer. In this case, they may turn to whatever information is most available at the time as long as it proves their point. Unfortunately, relying only on the information that is immediately available significantly reduces the risk of finding a solution that has a desirable outcome.

- Self-Serving bias- This bias describes the idea that people tend to take credit for success themselves while blaming outside factors for their failures. This bias makes it hard to truly identify the problem, which is an essential step when problem-solving.

#3: Start By Identifying the Problem

Once you can separate your personal bias from the facts, it becomes easier to identify the problem. When problem-solving, it can be useful to ask questions to clarify what the problem is. Asking questions can also help arrive at the source of the problem. Once the problem has been identified, it should be broken down until it is easy to understand.

#4: Visualize the Ideal Solution

Sometimes, it is easier to visualize a solution than to figure out the how. When you visualize the desired outcome, it gives you a destination that can be put on a roadmap. Now, you know where you started (the problem) and where you want to end (the ideal solution). Once the beginning and endpoints have been plotted, you can begin looking for routes that help you arrive there.

You should visualize the perfect solution with as much detail as possible, keeping in mind that not all solutions are going to end well. For example, if someone cheats on their spouse, they have the option of telling them or trying to hide it. Their ideal situation may be one where their partner forgives them for their indiscretion. Once they know they are seeking forgiveness, they may try to decide what to say to their partner that might make them more receptive to their message and forgiveness.

#5: Consider Possible Routes

Once you have all the information gathered, try to look at the problem and solution from different perspectives. Think about the possible courses of action and their potential risks and rewards. In some cases, you may find you need to combine more than one route to arrive at your destination.

As you consider possible options, use the mental models at your disposal to frame the situation in different ways. Each mental model presents a new way of looking at the problem—you just have to be familiar with which one to use. Using mental models for problem-solving is all about practice. As you familiarize yourself with the many tools in your toolbox, you'll find it is easier to know which models to choose for the problems you face.

Chapter 9:

Knowing When Mental Models Have Outlived Their Usefulness

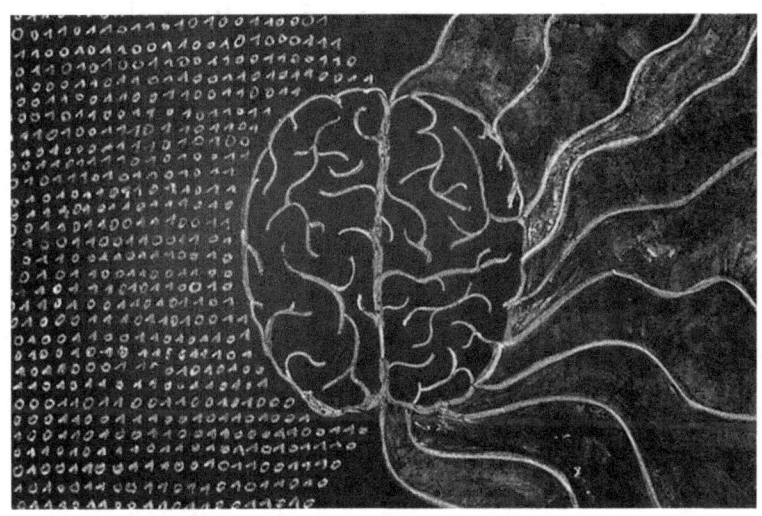

Mental models become a powerful tool when a person learns to identify them and apply them to problems and decisions. However, it is not uncommon for people to hold onto mental models that are no longer useful. For example, the Atlantic slave trade ended over 100 years ago. Even so, the devastating effects have left the entire area on guard. People are still cautious today because they have been taught to remain cautious and on guard.

Before you can overcome erroneous mental models or mental models that have outlived their usefulness, you'll have to identify them. This can be a challenge, as many people have a mental block against those things that disprove their core beliefs. This chapter will go over some of the ways that mental models can be flawed, so you can more critically evaluate which mental models to keep, which to build on, and which to replace with more effective models.

Attention and Perception

Mental models affect focus. As mentioned earlier, Warren Buffett and Charlie Munger look for certain indicators that tell them a company has a chance of growth before making an investment. However, this focus means that they do not focus on other areas of the business and there is some risk of overlooking information.

Mental models affect what a person chooses to pay attention to and how they perceive the information they have available. It can even affect the information that is readily available in the mind. Additionally, many people fill in information that is consistent with whatever mental model they are most familiar with. For example, someone who has a general distrust for leaders or political members as being untrustworthy is more likely to collect information and use it to infer that a leader is acting unethically rather than to evaluate their politics. They may even take the information collected and re-evaluate it, actively working to remain consistent with that category (untrustworthiness) that they relate to political figures.

Breaking Traditions

Many beliefs cannot be tested alone, as many of people's beliefs are passed down by general society. For example, it was many years before countries accepted that people of African American descent could be good leaders. Likewise, women are not heavily involved at an upper leadership level because not all of society believes a woman is capable of leading. To disprove this idea, however, it must be tested at the societal level.

Societal beliefs trickle down through generations. When a parent does not trust the government, this same mistrust often trickles down through the generations. Even though children are free to choose their own beliefs, their parental influence can make it impossible for them to test this distrust at a societal level until many others are ready to test that belief. This is one of the reasons that it is considered such a feat when a country has its first woman leader or their first colored leader—it represents a shift in the attitudes through the entire country and a generation that is more accepting of change and the possibility that the mental models they have believed most of their lives need to be challenged.

Belief Traps

When a person believes something, it creates what is known as a belief trap. This trap prevents theories from ever being tested because the person believes their mental model on such a deep level. For example, after an economic collapse, people may be less likely to put money in a bank or rely on a financial institution. Even years after the initial event, this distrust may remain and a person might continue avoiding working with financial institutions. There is always a chance that they could work with the banks again and have incredible benefits, renewing their trust, but some people will not take that risk. People are naturally inclined to do those things that they are comfortable with rather than testing new waters.

As the stakes get higher, the likelihood that someone will take the risk of challenging their mental model decreases. For example, there are medical practices like genital mutilation that are generally disapproved by advanced countries. However, some countries tell mothers that failing to have a female's genitals mutilated can decrease the risk of fertility or that it can be harmful or fatal in some way if the procedure is not done. Even though we know in the developed world that the practice is barbaric, it takes a brave mother to challenge the idea and risk harm to her female baby. Another bizarre habit practiced in some countries is tooth extraction for newborns where undeveloped baby teeth are removed to avoid contamination or sickness. Parents often do not believe they have the ability to challenge doctors—they just want their baby to get better and there is an authority telling them that is the way. Additionally, there is the risk (and guilt) associated with forgoing the medical procedure and risking something happening to their little one or their baby's illness getting worse. Even though there could be a great reward (avoiding a painful and unnecessary medical procedure), this comes with great risk.

Confirmation Bias and Ideology

Nobody likes to be told they are wrong. The human ego often interacts with the brain in a way that makes people suppress, forget, or ignore any observations that do not align with their core ideologies. Likewise, confirmation bias causes people to search for and use that information that supports their own core beliefs, rather than looking for balanced or new information that might prove the contrary.

The human tendency to disregard new and useful information in light of remaining 'right' in their beliefs is a major roadblock to success. Think of it this way—are you successful in your life right now? As successful as you want to be? Odds are, you still have goals that you want to reach and other things to do before you achieve success, whether at work or in your personal life. This version of success cannot be brought about without change. To change, people must be willing to accept new information and observe it critically, rather than allow bias to consider tainting their view of the world.

Additionally, some people struggle with confirmation bias because they have not shared the experience of someone else. For example, in the United States, sexual harassment is a problem in the workplace. Even so, many women do not speak up because they are afraid of losing their jobs, not being believed by general society, or other consequences. This happens because as a whole, society is made to believe that sexual harassment is not a problem and the women who do experience it is outliers. When women share their experiences, others have trouble understanding them or accepting that communication. Therefore, the woman does not have her concerns validated and the bias continues on.

Changing Mental Models on a Larger Level

One of the biggest obstacles when using mental models to interpret the world for a certain purpose is that the world and societal views deeply influence mental models, especially across gender and social castes. In Malawi, for example, it is not uncommon for women farmers to be disregarded when they bring their ideas forward, as they are considered less knowledgeable than men even though they have the same knowledge base. This happens in India too, when even educated women are considered less credible than their male counterparts.

On the opposite side, government policies can help shift public attitudes away from issues derived from stereotypes. For example, even after slavery ended in the United States, segregation remained a problem until it was eliminated. Even after the policies, however, there was an obstacle in the mental models and general negative attitude that some people continue to have towards people of a different skin color. This is not something based on fact in most cases, just a thought that has been passed down without being challenged through generations of people. The likelihood that someone will have racist beliefs is stronger in certain areas. However, this more than likely stems from the fact that people who like people who they see as similar to them. When they allow a person's skin color to influence their opinion more than someone's personality, they are limiting themselves by failing to notice the obvious similarities that we all share as humans.

Of course, policies change as attitudes shift. These policies can come from a government level but may also be influenced by the media. In India, for example, policies have shifted the way that women are treated in politics. In West Bengal, however, one village created a political affirmative action for women that allowed them the opportunity t lead for the first time. As this was implemented across different villages, it led to more women leading. After seven years, male attitudes were re-evaluated to see if they had shifted. Even though men still had a preference of male to female leaders, they were assured by female leaders who met certain standards and were considered competent leaders. In addition to influencing the way males viewed women leaders, the change in policy (and mental models) shifted society as a whole. Parents had new aspirations for their teenage daughters, adolescent females had a higher aspiration for themselves, and the gender gap in schooling in India narrowed slightly.

Even though the case in India represents a positive occurrence, unfortunately, the policy does not always take hold this way. In another village in India, political affirmative action was used to encourage teachers with a lower social status to run for village government. Unfortunately, this had the negative effect of increasing absenteeism in higher-caste teachers, which also increased negative outcomes in village schools. This was brought about by the resistance from high-caste teachers as they resisted the change that was being brought about.

The media can also affect a person's mental models. For example, overpopulation is a problem in many countries. More than likely, this trend comes from high birth rates from families that follow the cultural tradition of having larger families with many children. The study increased exposure to the idea by exposing communities to highly engaging soap operas. These soap operas were focused heavily on families with fewer children. Over the years, fertility rates declined. This same technique was applied across many municipalities in Brazil, effectively reducing fertility rates.

One of the most influential methods of changing mental models is early childhood intervention. Studies have shown that the education system can be used to shape a child's views on the world. For example, when children are encouraged to engage in classroom discussions and interact with classmates and their teacher, it can increase their level of trust, especially for people in their social group.

How to Change Your Personal Mental Models

As you learn more about those mental models in your life that no longer serve you, it is important to continue growing your collection and adding those models that offer benefits. The first step is challenging those mental models that do not serve you. Even though racism is generally accepted as wrong, people who were raised by racist parents have more trouble overcoming their aversion to people of a different skin color.

The key to changing mental models that do not serve you is starting at a different point in the process. Often, the mental models that are most damaging are those that are triggered instantly and cause action. Every decision goes through a cycle that includes:

- Taking actions that align with your beliefs
- Adopting beliefs about the world
- Drawing conclusions
- Making assumptions according to meaning
- Adding personal and cultural meanings to information
- Selection observed information
- Observing experiences and information

This cycle is a constant loop. Many people deal with their mental models at the top, where they have already been inspired to action. However, it is most effective to jump into this loop at the bottom. Here, when you are observing information and experiences, you have the power to consciously change what you pay attention to. Instead of quickly assigning information to what you are seeing and experiencing, it is important to take a step back and look at it from another perspective. Then, you can use the new information to incite change.

There are several ways to break this cycle. You can:

- Be aware of thoughts and possible fallacies in reasoning by asking questions about our own beliefs
- Use examples, facts, and information gathering to support a newer, more desirable mental model
- Ask about others' thinking and challenge our own point of view
- Interpret meaning for ourselves rather than making assumptions
- Align thoughts with our core beliefs and self-expression

You should never be afraid to question your beliefs. In fact, questioning beliefs is one element that can help you overcome your beliefs. Find out if what you believe is based on fact or assumption. Then, allow your internal dialogue to help you tackle complex problems. It can also be helpful to dialogue with someone else who has different core beliefs, particularly once you are open to a new way of thinking and willing to listen to their unique perspective. Then, take the time to reflect on your thoughts, feelings, and behaviors. As you realize the relationship between these things, you'll learn the effects of your thoughts, feelings, and behaviors on your own circumstances and the world around you.

Once you have accepted that a mental model no longer serves you, it will take time to overcome your initial assumptions. When you make decisions or solve problems, take the time to be sure these assumptions are not affecting your ability to have clear thoughts. It will take conscious effort for some time and careful evaluation of your thoughts. As you continue to consciously refute the unwanted mental model and disprove it, your mind will notice your efforts and eventually change that pathway of thinking.

Conclusion

Mental models can serve us or hinder us as we make decisions, solve problems, and go about our day-to-day lives. The key to using mental models is choosing the right model for the right scenario. Often, this involves overlapping models from different disciplines, which allows you the chance to see things from a new perspective. Before you can begin using these different mental models, however, you must first master them and understand the full range of their abilities, as well any restrictions that may exist.

Hopefully, this book has helped you understand how mental models can change the way you think. As you gain more control of your thoughts, feelings, and behaviors, you gain more control in your life. Ultimately, you'll have the power to make the decisions and overcome obstacles to success, giving you the opportunity to achieve any goal that you set in life.

People like Warren Buffett, Charlie Munger, Jeff Bezos, and Elon Musk have all relied on a variety of mental models through their lifetimes, which has helped them shape their success. By studying the key principles in different disciplines and using this unique approach, you'll find yourself able to consistently make choices and solve problems in a way that allows for good outcomes. As your good outcomes increase, so does the quality of your life.

Thank you for reading and best of luck!

References

http://mentalmodels.princeton.edu/about/what-are-mental-models/

https://fs.blog/mental-models/

https://jamesclear.com/feynman-mental-models

https://medium.com/personal-growth/charlie-munger-how-to-get-smarter-by-using-mental-models-4659fe6d53db

https://www.brainyquote.com/quotes/elizabeth_thornton_735226

http://robdkelly.com/blog/mental-models/attribution-theory-in-busines/

http://www.focusinvestor.com/FocusSeriesPart3.pdf

http://robdkelly.com/blog/mental-models/autocatalysis-in-business/

http://robdkelly.com/blog/mental-models/a-list-of-top-100-mental-models-for-business/

https://medium.com/accelerated-intelligence/learn-like-elon-musk-fe8f8da6137c

https://alyjuma.com/regret-minimization-framework/

https://www.investopedia.com/terms/t/timevalueofmoney.asp

http://pubdocs.worldbank.org/en/504271482349886430/Chapter-3.pdf

https://www.mymentalmodels.info/what-are-mental-models/

https://www.mymentalmodels.info/redundancy-in-engineering/

https://fs.blog/2013/01/mental-model-equilibrium/

https://medium.com/personal-growth/mental-models-898f70438075

http://info.marshall.usc.edu/faculty/critthink/Supplemental%20Material/Reducing%20Bias.pdf

https://corporatefinanceinstitute.com/resources/knowledge/trading-investing/framing-bias/

https://gothamculture.com/2017/03/23/challenge-mental-models-think-differently/

https://www.rationalpov.com/mentalmodel/autocatalysis/

https://www.thebalancecareers.com/pareto-s-principle-the-80-20-rule-2275148

http://robdkelly.com/blog/mental-models/cumulative-advantage-the-matthew-effect/

https://www.thebalancecareers.com/pareto-s-principle-the-80-20-rule-2275148

https://fs.blog/2016/08/multiplicative-systems/

https://www.rypeapp.com/blog/how-to-improve-decision-making-skill/

https://fs.blog/2011/08/the-tragedy-of-the-commons/

https://fs.blog/2017/08/the-butterfly-effect/

https://sevenwaysoflearning.com/the-seven-ways/learning-with-mental-models/

https://lifehacker.com/mental-models-solve-problems-by-approaching-them-from-1682835620

https://fs.blog/2017/06/activation-energy/

https://fs.blog/2014/04/mental-model-complex-adaptive-systems/

https://fs.blog/2018/03/speed-velocity/

https://fs.blog/2017/06/leverage/

https://fs.blog/2017/10/bias-incentives-reinforcement/

www.ingramcontent.com/pod-product-compliance
Lightning Source LLC
Chambersburg PA
CBHW072144280526
45788CB00002B/773